S0-CDO-633

Bulls and Bears

Winning in the Stock Market in Good Times and Bad

HUGH ANDERSON

THE GLOBE AND MAIL

Penguin Books

PENGUIN BOOKS
Published by the Penguin Group
Penguin Books Canada Ltd., 10 Alcorn Avenue, Suite 300, Toronto, Canada, M4V 3B2
Penguin Books Ltd., 27 Wrights Lane, London W8 5TZ, England
Viking Penguin Inc., 40 West 23rd Street, New York, New York 10010, USA
Penguin Books Australia Ltd., Ringwood, Victoria, Australia
Penguin Books (NZ) Ltd., 182-190 Wairau Road, Auckland 10, New Zealand
Penguin Books Ltd., Registered Offices: Harmondsworth, Middlesex, England
Published in Penguin Books 1996

10 9 8 7 6 5 4 3 2 1

Copyright © Globe Information Services, 1996
All inquiries should be addressed to Globe Information Services, 444 Front Street
West, Toronto, Ontario M5V 2S9 (416) 585-5250.

All rights reserved. Except in the United States of America, this book is sold subject
to the condition that it shall not, by way of trade or otherwise, be lent, re-sold, hired
out, or otherwise circulated without the publisher's prior consent in any form of
binding or cover other than that in which it is published and without a similar condition, including this condition, being imposed on the subsequent purchaser.

Canadian Cataloguing in Publication Data
The National Library of Canada has catalogued this publication as follows.
Anderson, Hugh, 1935 –
    Bulls and bears
(Financial Times personal finance library)
Annual.
[1990]-
At head of title: Financial Times, 1993-1995; The Globe and Mail, 1996-
Following title: Winning in the stock market in good times and bad.
Issues for 1996- ... published in the series: The Globe and Mail personal finance li-
brary.
ISSN 1193-8986
ISBN 0-14-026257-1 (1996)
1. Stocks – Periodicals. 2. Stock-exchange – Periodicals. 3. Investments – Peri-
odicals. I. Title. II. Title: Financial Times. III. Title: Globe and Mail. IV. Title: Financial
Times of Canada. V. Series. VI. Series: The Globe and Mail personal finance library.

HG4551.A64   332.63'22'05   C93-030706-2

Cover design: Creative Network
Cover illustration: Peter Yundt
Charts: Ivy Wong
The information contained in this book is intended only as a general guide and may
not be suitable for certain individuals. If expert advice is warranted, readers are
urged to consult a competent professional. While the legal, tax and accounting information contained in this book has been obtained from sources believed to be accurate, constant changes in the legal and financial environment make it imperative
that readers confirm this information before making financial decisions.

CONTENTS

APPENDICES

Tables and Illustrations

CHARTS

TABLES

Dedication

To my children, Colin and Sarah, with love and the hope they may profit from advice in this book from time to time.

Acknowledgements

My grateful thanks to:

Johanne Duc, my assistant, who found some needed information for me and dealt ably with clients' calls in my absence while I worked on this new edition.

Mark Lazarus, my brother-in-law the broker, who enlightened me frequently on the practical details of his difficult trade but broke no confidences.

Ron Meisels, one of Canada's top technical analysts, who laboured long and hard to ensure that I really understood his trade. If I still didn't, it is not his fault.

Bill Ram, a thoughtful and independent-minded broker in a business that does not always encourage such qualities, with whom I have discussed many of the ideas in this book.

Sydney Sweibel, an able tax lawyer who spent considerable time improving my understanding of our ridiculously complicated tax rules. Again, it is not his fault if I still got it wrong.

Claire Stevens, an able accountant, who keeps me up to date on constantly changing tax rates and rules that affect investors.

Introduction

"MONEY MAKES MONEY," I used to hear them say in the north of England, where I grew up. This is a book designed to help people make that prophecy come true for themselves by having their money make more money in the stock market. It is for those who have already put something aside for emergencies and the other basics of personal financial management. It is also for those who hope to be able to reach that point in the not-too-distant future. It is even for those who have already risked some of their savings in the stock market, perhaps with unhappy results.

All of these people have a common problem: Idle money is wasted money. Dollars not spent on food, housing, fun and the other daily expenses of living shrink in value with amazing speed if they are allowed to sit around doing nothing. At a historically moderate inflation rate of 5 per cent, a dollar's purchasing power drops to 61 cents in a decade. Add to that the fact that by making the modest effort needed to park that dollar in a virtually risk-free term deposit, you could have it bring in something like 7 per cent in interest a year. If you can keep doing that each year, leaving the 7 per cent alone to earn more interest, the dramatic power of compound interest will turn one dollar into two in little more than 10 years, putting you comfortably ahead of inflation, at least before taxes.

This is what investing is about. Dollars you save must be used to make more dollars if you are to get ahead of the game, or even to stay more or less in the same place. But there are many ways to invest, and some require less time and effort than the stock market. So why bother with stocks? Life is short, after all, and there is much to enjoy.

The answer is that your dollars can grow more quickly from successful investment in the stock market than from savings deposits, government and corporate bonds, or most other investments. Over the 28 years from 1966 to 1995, which included some years of unusually high interest rates and some dismaying stock market declines, the average annual return on representative stocks still outstripped what you could have earned on interest-paying investments. The comparison assumes that all dividends and interest payments were reinvested, which is the smart thing to do because it puts compounding to work on your behalf. Comparisons over the last half-dozen decades reinforce the point. In addition, if you invest in Canadian stocks, you often do better after tax than from investing to earn interest payments. That's because income earned from dividends and capital gains is not taxed as heavily as interest income.

You should note, however, that there are no guarantees of success in the stock market. No form of investment is without risk, and the stock market is riskier than many. Yet those who invest smartly in stocks can do very well. For example, if you had bought Canadian Imperial Bank of Commerce shares at about $32 in August, 1995, and sold them at around their high of $46.65 in May, 1996, you would have made 50 per cent on your money in less than a year in a blue-chip investment. Buy stocks without rhyme or reason, though, and you can lose your savings in a hurry. Pile into a hot stock like Newbridge because of the media hype about the company's prospects, as many did in May, 1996, when the stock sold for as much as $102, and you could still be holding on for dear life two months later as it careened downward toward $60.

This book encourages you to take the time and trouble to invest intelligently in the stock market by making the final decisions yourself. But is this really a good idea for you? It's a good question and one that deserves a serious answer. After all, if there's carpentry to be done, only a few people will try to do it themselves. The water pipes need fixing? Call a plumber. Got a legal problem? Go to a lawyer. Need to fly to another city? You don't go out and get a pilot's licence; you rent a seat on a plane flown by professionals.

What's more, the stock market is a tough arena. Many of the players are as smart as you, and some are smarter. If you're a beginner, most everybody else has more experience. Many of your rivals have bigger bankrolls, too.

So if you have spare money that you would like to use to make more money, perhaps the smart move is to find and pay some experts to make all the decisions for you. It's not hard. There are hundreds of them out there, beseeching you to give them the chance to invest your money. There are mutual fund salesmen, stockbrokers, personal financial planners, insurance salesmen, bankers and trust company executives, all offering you the prospect of greater wealth if only you entrust your savings totally to their skillful and experienced hands.

There's a fee to be paid, of course. Run quickly away from any would-be adviser who suggests there isn't. The reputable experts won't deny it. If asked, they will point out that free advice is worth about what it costs and that they have to earn a living, too. But what's a few dollars here and there if spending them will help make you wealthy? Does a lottery winner begrudge the cash spent on losing tickets before the big payout?

These are persuasive arguments, but they are not totally convincing. There is a good reason for taking the time and trouble to learn how to win in the stock market while staying in control yourself. It's because no one cares about your money as much as you do. Expert advisers may say they care that much. They may even believe what they say. But if you learn nothing else from the experience, your first venture into the market should teach you that it makes a huge difference when it's your own money that's on the line.

To yourself, you are an important person. It is said that the prospect of being hanged in the morning concentrates the mind wonderfully. It's also true that the prospect of losing some of your savings, usually acquired with much pain and effort, has a way of getting your close attention. People who can hardly remember their spouse's birthday can recall with impressive accuracy the day-to-day ups and downs in the prices of stocks they own and quickly calculate the consequences for their personal wealth.

To a professional adviser, you are just another customer. Of course, a good adviser will give your money his or her best shot because that's the way to stay in business. Almost certainly, you will do better following an expert's advice if you are not prepared to invest sufficient time and attention to give it a good shot yourself. Venturing into the stock market with little investment knowledge can be much like playing a tennis match against Steffi Graf without some natural talent, a lot of coaching and hours of practice. The match is likely to end quickly and you are not going to have much fun. The only uncertainty is by what margin you will lose.

It's also true that success in the stock market can sometimes seem a random thing, a result of blind luck or the right connections.

When most stocks are rising in price, the world seems full of people who did well in the market without knowing much about what they were doing. But check with those people when most stock prices are moving down and you will almost certainly find them more subdued, even chastened, by the experience of losing — and frequently ignorant about why things went wrong.

Take the trouble to learn about investing and you can do better. Certainly, you should still be willing to listen to the advice of experts you trust, but you will be better equipped to assess the value of their advice. You may even beat the professionals if you make the effort and pay close enough attention. There is a wealth of evidence that professional investment managers, on average, don't do much better than the rest of us, on average.

Success isn't easy, of course. If it were, we would all be rich. Some natural talent also helps. But it's perfectly possible to beat the professionals at their own game and walk away from the table with more than you had when you started. What's more, making the calls yourself is more fun, especially when you win.

Reading this book will teach you the basics of investing in the stock market. You will learn what the market is and why people care about it. You'll meet the bulls and the bears and some of the other key characters. You will learn about market cycles and about the methods used by investors to make sense of the market and to plan their strategies. You will encounter some of the more exotic forms of stock market investment, learn how the taxman's rules can help and hurt you, and how to keep score of how you are doing. Finally, you will learn of the importance of psychology in the market and the need to know yourself in order to win. You'll also be offered some thoughts on how the stock market is likely to fare in the remainder of this century.

This knowledge will provide a solid launching pad for your self-reliant adventure in the stock market. That is exactly how you should regard it — as an adventure, not a grim struggle. The stock market must be wooed and won, not conquered. It has a way of punishing arrogant players just when they feel triumphant. It rewards smartness tempered with sensitivity to the mysteries of human nature. You will need the fortitude to live with your inevitable mistakes and the humility to realize that your successes may be only partly the result of your own brilliance.

Good wooing!

CHAPTER 1

Why the Stock Market Matters

WATCH ANY TELEVISION newscast, listen to the car radio on your way home, glance at the morning paper as you pour milk on your breakfast cereal, and the chances are that somebody will be talking about the stock market. Was the Dow Jones average down 50 points yesterday? That's bad, and if it happens again today, we're in for big trouble. Has Toronto climbed 75 points in the first two hours of trading today? Good times are here again. What's that about the Tokyo market? It's off 200 points? Not to worry, that sort of move doesn't mean much in Tokyo. It will bounce back tomorrow. How did stocks open in London this morning? Strongly? That's good. Things are picking up over there, aren't they?

Just what is this thing called the stock market, and why do so many people care what's happening to it? You can see a part of the stock market in action if you visit the Toronto Stock Exchange on a regular working day and ask to be directed to the public gallery. Looking down from there, you will see a large room filled with people — mostly men — sometimes shouting at each other, sometimes moving purposefully across the floor, sometimes gazing pensively at indicator screens scattered around the room, or sometimes just seemingly standing around. Every now and then, somebody will scribble on a small piece of paper and hand it to a clerk who will enter information into a computer terminal. Similar scenes can be observed on the trading floors of the Montreal and Vancouver exchanges, and at the New York Stock Exchange on world-famous Wall Street.

That piece of paper and the information entered into the computer are the heart of the matter. They record the fact that an investor has bought or sold some shares, or maybe the right to buy or sell some shares later on from another investor. The transaction may involve 100 shares of Air Canada, one of the most widely owned companies in Canada. In that case, the investors involved were probably small-time players. On the other hand, it might involve 100,000 shares of Imperial Oil, Canada's biggest oil company, and the investors involved will probably be professional managers of large amounts of other people's money. In either case, some shares in a company will be changing hands, from one investor to another. The job of the people milling around on the exchange trading floor is to get their customers the best available price in a sort of continuous auction sale — the lowest price for a buyer and the highest for a seller.

For every buyer in the stock market, a seller has been found at a mutually acceptable price. Otherwise, no transaction would have taken place. There can never be more buyers than sellers, although some careless commentary suggests so. What there can be is more anxious buyers than sellers and, as everybody who has bargained with a car dealer learns, anxious buyers usually pay more. At such a time average prices of shares will rise. The more anxious, or eager, the buyers are, the faster and further prices will climb. This much-welcomed state of affairs is what is meant when people talk about a "bull" market.

Conversely, if the sellers are more anxious than the buyers, prices will fall, on average, because the sellers are willing to accept less to get rid of their shares. The stock market offers the world's most highly publicized demonstration of the law of supply and demand in action, a show that takes place every day except weekends and holidays. When there is more supply than demand — in other words, the sellers are eager and the buyers are cautious — this less welcome state of affairs is called a "bear" market.

Alert newcomers may sense an opportunity in this ebb and flow of the stock market, and they would be right. Much money can be made by buying at low prices from anxious sellers, then selling at high prices to eager buyers. The trick is to avoid doing it the other way round — that is, buying high and selling low. Unhappily, it's not as easy as it sounds, although this book should help you get it right.

Buying and selling in the stock market is done on the grand scale. In 1995, a good year for the business, some $257 billion worth of transactions took place on the five major Canadian stock exchanges: Toronto, Montreal, Vancouver, Alberta and Winnipeg. A total of 27.2 billion shares changed hands during the year.

This is big business. Canada's stockbrokers were paid about $2.6 billion in commissions in 1995 to handle those transactions, an average of about 1 per cent. That's not as much as the 6 per cent you often pay a real estate broker to sell your house but it's still a figure worth remembering. Those commissions were paid by investors whether they were buying or selling, at a loss or at a profit. So long as people are buying or selling, the broker gets a commission. The problem for brokers is that in a bear market, when stock prices are mostly falling, people shy away from investing. That's not healthy for a business that thrives on optimism. Pessimistic investors, however, can do well when the times demand pessimism. You must not be an optimist or a pessimist for all seasons, however strong the temptation.

The curious thing about all this buying and selling is that when you have bought and paid for your shares, you don't get anything as tangible as a house or a car. The only thing you can touch is usually a printed share certificate, and frequently you don't get even that.

What you do get of value is the legal right to share in the fortunes of the company whose shares you own, just like such big-time businessmen as Kenneth Thomson, Edgar Bronfman or Conrad Black. You, too, can be a capitalist and own a piece of corporate Canada or corporate America, or wherever your fancy has taken your money. Don't get carried away, though. It's unlikely that an investment of a few thousand dollars will buy you a seat in the company's boardroom. You will not be consulted before a new business strategy is adopted or a takeover bid launched. You will not be asked for your opinion on how to clean up that costly problem in the European division. You can, however, be reasonably sure of civil treatment by the company's top management and directors if you show up at the annual meeting of shareholders. You are also entitled by law to a regular flow of information about how the company is doing and why.

Even better, in many cases you will start to receive regular dividend cheques, sometimes twice a year and frequently four times a year. This is usually the most immediate financial reward you get for risking your hard-saved capital in the stock market, unless you get lucky and the company is bought out two weeks later for 20 per cent more than you paid for your shares. Not all companies pay dividends to their shareholders, however, and some that did have since stopped while they struggle through hard times. This is the most important thing to remember about dividends: They come out of the company's profits. So, if the company isn't doing well, they may stop coming.

If you buy shares in a company such as BCE Inc., which has paid dividends every year for 114 years, it's easy to think of them as equivalent to the interest payments you receive through your bank savings account or on a government savings bond. They are not. When a company or a government offers to pay interest on money it wants to borrow, it promises to make the payments, come what may. A company that invites you to buy its stock makes no such legally binding promise to pay dividends. In that case, the payments are entirely at the discretion of the company's directors.

Why do companies decide to sell shares to outsiders like you, and pay dividends out of the profits when they can and when they want to? In fact, most don't. They stay as private companies, raising capital by selling shares to a small group of investors, or perhaps to only one. They conduct themselves like private clubs which keep control of how many members they want and what kind. But the shares of many companies, including some of the world's biggest and best known, can be owned by anybody who will pay the price. These companies first "go public" with an offer of new shares to all comers. The money they get for the shares, less expenses, goes into the company's treasury and boosts its capital. Then the new shares are traded on the stock market by anybody who wants to play.

After the initial sale of new shares, none of the money paid by buyers goes to the company. It goes to the previous owner of the shares. That being the case, there may seem to be nothing for the company in the continued public trading of its shares. Unlike private companies, public companies have to tell the outside world a great deal about their affairs. When business goes badly, their directors and executives face the added indignity of having their performance commented on and criticized by anybody who pays attention to the information they are obliged to disclose. Because the price of the company's stock is considered one measure of their success or failure, they face a public referendum every business day on how they are doing. Going public hardly makes sense, does it?

Clearly, this isn't so. Indeed, many companies value public trading in their shares so highly that they willingly take on the additional obligations and costs of listing their shares on a stock exchange. Here are some of the advantages:

Canada's 15 Largest Public Companies

BY MARKET CAPITALIZATION ON AUGUST 29, 1996

Company	Common shares outstanding (millions)*	Share price ($)	Market capitalization ($ millions)
Northern Telecom Limited	254.4	69.25	17,613,985
The Seagram Co. Ltd.	374.5	45.65	17,094,190
BCE Inc.	313.8	54.00	16,946,315
The Thomson Corporation	594.7	24.30	14,451,994
Barrick Gold Corporation	357.2	37.40	13,359,280
Imperial Oil Limited	189.0	58.90	11,132,720
Royal Bank of Canada	314.2	34.55	10,854,054
Canadian Pacific Limited	342.3	30.95	10,594,185
Canadian Imperial Bank of Commerce	216.3	45.90	9,930,236
Alcan Aluminium Limited	225.9	43.30	9,782,033
Bank of Montreal	263.7	33.75	8,899,354
The Toronto Dominion Bank	301.4	26.45	7,972,098
Placer Dome Inc.	239.1	33.05	7,901,928
The Bank of Nova Scotia	232.3	34.00	7,896,718
Noranda Inc.	231.8	28.75	6,664,394

*shares outstanding as of latest annual report
All amounts converted to Canadian dollars.

SOURCE: GLOBE INFORMATION SERVICES

TABLE I

• The sale of new shares through a public offering is usually the cheapest source of capital for a company, despite the incidental expenses. That's because it's usually done when it's possible to put a high price on the new shares. And once done successfully, it can be done again and again. Money can also be raised conveniently and on good terms from existing shareholders by giving them "rights" to buy more shares at a discount from the market price.

• For companies in lines of business that benefit from widespread public recognition, a stock exchange listing is a sort of seal of approval. The company is likely to attract more shareholders because buying and selling of its stock becomes easier, and satisfied shareholders are likely to become customers and unpaid sales representatives for its products.

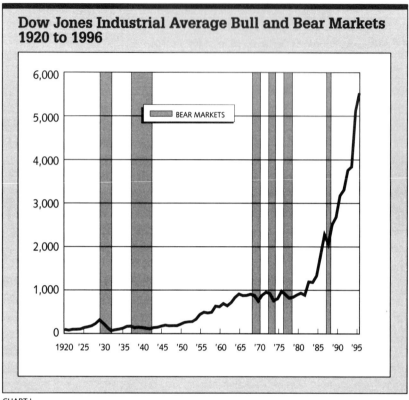

Dow Jones Industrial Average Bull and Bear Markets 1920 to 1996

BEAR MARKETS

CHART I

• A publicly quoted price for a company's shares makes it easier to swing mergers or other deals that require an up-to-date and accepted valuation of the company. It also makes it easier for shareholders to arrange loans using the shares as security. Employees also feel more comfortable with stock-purchase options whose value can be followed on a daily basis.

Companies that want Canadian investors and meet the listing requirements have the choice of three major Canadian stock exchanges and two minor ones. The country's biggest exchange is the Toronto Stock Exchange, which handles more than three-quarters of the value of listed stock-trading business in Canada. The shares of some 1,200 companies were listed in Toronto in mid-1996. Toronto's closest rival is the Montreal Exchange, with roughly 15 per cent of the business and some 500 companies with shares listed. Number three is the Vancouver Stock Exchange, with 3 per cent of the business and some 2,000 companies listed. The two minor ex-

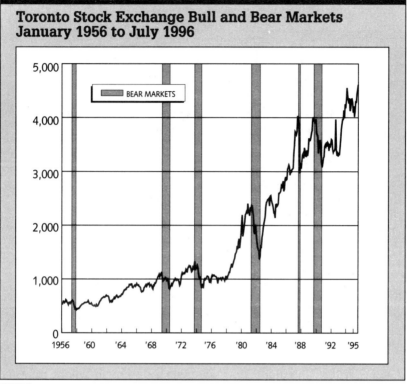

Toronto Stock Exchange Bull and Bear Markets
January 1956 to July 1996

BEAR MARKETS

CHART II

changes are the Alberta Stock Exchange in Calgary and the almost
invisible Winnipeg Stock Exchange.

The Toronto Stock Exchange attracts most of the major public
companies in all Canadian industries, as well as many smaller ones.
Many companies list their shares only in Toronto but big firms that
want national visibility list in Montreal and Vancouver, too. Que-
bec-based public companies, big and small, usually list their shares
in Montreal, although some list in Toronto and Vancouver as well.
Vancouver has some big companies but its list predominantly consists of lower-priced stocks of companies in the business of mining
exploration or searching for oil and gas. Alberta's list consists principally of stocks of oil and gas exploration companies.

Each Canadian exchange has some stocks of foreign companies,
those with an interest in attracting Canadian investors or Canadian
customers. Conversely, Canadian investors are not restricted to buying and selling on the Canadian exchanges. The whole world is

open to you, including the world's biggest and best-known stock exchange, on New York's Wall Street. The number and value of shares
traded on the New York Stock Exchange dwarf the Toronto totals,
and the choice of industries in which you can invest is the widest
in the world. Most of the time, the action on Wall Street sets the
tone for the stock market throughout the world and especially in
Canada. If stock prices are rising in New York, the odds are they
will be rising here. If prices are falling in New York, they are likely
to be weak here.

If you want to trade stocks in the early hours of the morning, you
can have your stockbroker arrange transactions on stock exchanges
in London or Paris. If you are a night owl, you can do the same
thing in Tokyo or Hong Kong, which get going after North America
closes down. However, most Canadian investors don't venture that
far afield. While many buy stocks listed in New York and on other
U.S. stock exchanges, only a handful are prepared to tackle the
problems of keeping in touch with what's happening in Europe and
the Far East, plus the risks of losing whatever they may win when
converting local currency back into Canadian dollars. Similarly, and
wisely, only a small minority venture among the huge number of
stocks that are not traded on any stock exchange. These change
hands on the "unlisted" stock markets — a jungle where information about what is going on, and why, is hard to come by and frequently misleading.

Wherever you buy stocks, it's a pleasant reward when dividends
start arriving regularly. Then there's the added benefit of having
dividend income from Canadian companies treated by the taxman
in a less demanding way than your regular pay. But cashing dividend cheques is not the way to win big in the stock market. The appeal in shares traded on the market lies in the possibility that you
can sell them to somebody else for a lot more than you paid for
them, after commissions. This is what's meant by a capital gain and
the taxman in most circumstances treats the fruits of such success
almost as generously as dividend payments.

There is a catch. Prices of company shares do go down now and
then, usually just after many of us have bought them. So it is possible, or even inevitable, that from time to time you will sell shares to
somebody else for less than you paid for them. This is known as a
capital loss, and it's one of the more depressing aspects of investing
in the stock market. But there is some comfort in the fact that the

taxman allows you to offset your capital gains with your capital losses, within limits, when you calculate your tax bill. This means the government shares the cost of your misfortune.

Clearly, it is easier to avoid capital losses if you begin investing in the stock market when the odds are with you, rather than against you — that is, during a strong bull market, when the majority of stocks are rising in price. At such times it's easy to get the idea you are a financial genius. "How long has this been going on and why didn't I know about it sooner?" you may ask yourself as you buy stocks and watch them go up. Don't be fooled, though. Bear markets play nasty tricks on fledgling financial geniuses and as sure as winter succeeds summer, every bull market is sooner or later followed by the other kind. Since 1920, there have been eight officially recognized bull markets and seven bear markets. The last 56 years have seen 39 in which most stocks rose in price and 17 years in which the prices of most stocks fell. Remember also that you are always playing the odds. Even during a bull market the prices of some stocks fall.

Why does this constant ebb and flow occur? This is supposed to be the century of progress, isn't it? Why can't the stock market always progress in an upward direction? The answer lies in the fact that the economy does not constantly progress. From time to time it gets sick — sometimes suffering the economic equivalent of a mild flu, on other occasions a raging fever and at least once in this century an almost total collapse, known as the Great Depression. During such times of economic sickness, the business fortunes of companies whose shares are traded on the stock market worsen. Orders for products and services shrink or disappear. Profits suffer a similar fate. Employees are laid off. Executives lose their big paycheques and fancy perks. A bad time is had by all, and worried investors are no longer willing to pay high prices for company shares. Fear overwhelms greed.

In fact, investors usually try to anticipate trouble and unload their holdings before disaster arrives. Economists are paid big money by professional investment managers to peer into the future and give advance warning of problems such as economic recessions. They are also expected to provide advance warning of the economy's return to health so clients can buy back into the market at low prices before everybody else realizes what is going on.

It doesn't always work, of course. Cynical players can be heard to observe that the market predicted 10 of the last five recessions. But investors who want to win should always be aware of whether the economic tide is coming in or is about to go out. Rowing against the tide is tougher than riding along with it, although sometimes it may be necessary to do just that.

CHAPTER 2

Finding
Your Way

IN A WAY, IT'S ALMOST TOO
easy to find out what's happening in the stock market. On week-
days, it's difficult to avoid knowing, whether you want to or not.
From the first radio news summary in the morning to the evening
television business wrap-up there's a constant flow of reports that
the market is up, down or sideways. Open your morning paper to
the business section and you'll find a story about what happened
yesterday. If the market moved far and fast, you may not even have
to turn to the business pages; the story may be on page 1. On the
weekend there will be background pieces, analysis and commentary, seeking to explain and make sense of it all. Then there are the
financial weeklies, with still more reporting, commentary and
analysis. There is also the minute-by-minute coverage on cable television, and *Nightly Business Report* and *Wall Street Week* on the
PBS television network.

With this vast amount of information, it would seem that anybody who pays only a modest amount of attention can follow the
daily ebb and flow of the market. That's not always the case,
though. This is one of those instances where information overload
can, and frequently does, overwhelm the ability of the receiver to
sort things out. A clear picture of what's happening is obscured by a
fog of often irrelevant, frequently contradictory reports. Rumours
and facts emerge cheek by jowl without the filtering that might help
you distinguish one from the other.

It's easy to tell fact from fiction in some cases. A climb of 50
points in the Dow Jones industrial average, the closely watched indicator of performance on the New York Stock Exchange, is a fact,
not a rumour, and one that is worth knowing. So is the information
that this was the first rise in two weeks. But these facts don't take us
very far. What do they really mean? Has a new bull market begun or

is the sudden upward move just a trap for the unwary? What's likely to happen next, and how can money be made?

The journalists who prepare daily summaries try to answer these more interesting questions. If some important economic statistic has just been published, such as the latest calculation of the inflation rate, they will seek comments from economists and professional stock market analysts about why the market rose as a result. The figure may have been smaller than expected, so the market could have risen on a collective sigh of relief. If a major corporate takeover bid was announced yesterday, the journalists will seek out analysts who may say the market rose because investors expect more takeover bids to be made at high prices. Such analysts may recommend that investors buy stocks before the market rises further. But other, more pessimistic, analysts, may say the rise gives investors a chance to get out at better prices than they could have a few days before and urge them to sell.

These comments will be faithfully reported, printed in newspapers across the country and broadcast far and wide on radio and television. Contradictions and all, they will become the published wisdom about what happened in the market yesterday — but surviving perhaps for only a few hours until it is realized that today the market is not behaving at all like it did yesterday. In the first hour of trading, the Dow Jones average is down 55 points, more than wiping out the previous day's gain. Clearly, yesterday's climb was merely a temporary interruption in the market's downward path. It's crazy to think the market will do well in the first year of a new U.S. president's term, isn't it? Everybody knows the new man makes all the tough moves early so voters will forget them before the next election four years later. Every journalist on the stock market beat knows some analyst who will come up with that sort of thing when asked. So the published wisdom will be fashioned to fit today's facts, which inconveniently turned out to be different from yesterday's.

If you want to win in the market, it's important not to pay too much attention to daily summaries. Find out whether the market is going up or down, and by how much, but skip the off-the-cuff reasoning. Take note of the news events that may affect the economic environment — a change in corporate tax rules that will have an impact on after-tax profits, a copper-industry strike in Chile that will mean higher prices and more business for Canadian copper producers, more disagreements between members of the Organization

Statistical trends

MARKET ECONOMY	Period	Latest	% Change From Prev.	Yr Ago
Gross domestic product/seasonally adj., annual rate, 1986 $bln	May	549.6	0.2	1.4
Merch. exports/seasonally adjusted, bal. of payments basis, $bln	May	22.4	2.9	7.9
Merch. imports/seasonally adjusted, bal. of payments basis, $bln	May	18.3	-2.1	-3.8
Retail trade/seasonally adjusted, $bln	May	17.8	0.0	1.1

	Period	Latest	Prev.	Yr Ago
Merch. trade balance/seasonally adj., bal. of payments basis, $mln	May	4,106.9	3,096.1	1,744.2
New car sales/seasonally adjusted, units, 000s	June	55.8	53.9	57.1
Housing starts/seasonally adjusted, annual rate, 000s	July	129	135	96
Unemployment rate/seasonally adjusted, %	July	9.8	10.0	9.7
Service employment/seasonally adjusted, mln	July	10.1	10.2	10.0
Goods-producing employment/seasonally adjusted, mln	July	3.5	3.5	3.5

FINANCIAL ECONOMY	Period	Latest	Prev.	Yr Ago
Dollar/weekly average, Toronto noon, U.S. cents	Last wk	72.80	72.89	73.54
Gold/weekly average, London afternoon fix, $U.S.	Last wk	386.90	388.42	384.52
Money supply, narrow/M-1, $bln, seasonally adjusted	June	64.3	63.9	60.0
Money supply, narrow/M-2, $bln, seasonally adjusted	June	390.7	389.9	379.9
Money supply, broad/M-3, $bln, seasonally adjusted	June	480.1	479.4	456.9
Business credit/seasonally adjusted, $bln	June	558.8	557.7	534.2
Household credit/seasonally adjusted, $bln	May	473.0	470.9	450.0
Treasury bills/Bank of Canada holdings, $bln	Last wk	19.7	19.8	17.7
Bonds/Bank of Canada holdings, $bln	Last wk	5.6	5.6	5.6
Canada Savings Bonds/outstanding, $bln	Last wk	30.1	30.2	29.6
Government of Canada cash balances/$bln	Last wk	5.3	6.9	8.3
Bank of Canada rate/%	Aug. 15	4.50	4.50	6.82
Treasury bill yield/91-day, %	Aug. 13	4.17	4.22	6.57
Chartered bank prime rate/%	Aug. 14	6.00	6.00	8.25
Canada bond yield/weighted long-term average, %	Aug. 15	7.62	7.62	8.60
Corporate bond yield/weighted long-term average, %	Aug. 14	8.15	8.19	9.28

PRICES	Period	Latest	% Change From Prev.	Yr Ago
Consumer price index/1986 = 100	July	135.6	0.0	1.2
Industrial production price index/1986 = 100	June	129.1	-0.4	-0.2
Raw materials price index/1986 = 100	June	134.6	-2.3	0.8

U.S. ECONOMY	Period	Latest	% Change From Prev.	Yr Ago
GDP/seasonally adjusted, annual rate, 1987 $bln (Advance)	2Q	6,885.1	1.0	2.6
Merch. exports/seasonally adjusted, f.a.s. basis, $bln	May	52.4	1.6	7.4
Merch. imports/seasonally adjusted, c.v. basis, $bln	May	66.9	3.4	6.3
Consumer price index/1982-1984 = 100/seasonally adjusted	July	157.2	0.3	2.9

	Period	Latest	Prev.	Yr Ago
Merch. trade balance/seasonally adjusted, c.v. basis, $bln	May	-14.5	−13.1	−14.1
Unemployment rate/seasonally adjusted, %	July	5.4	5.3	5.7
Federal reserve discount rate/%	Last wk	5.00	5.00	5.25

SOURCE: THE GLOBE AND MAIL

TABLE II

of Petroleum Exporting Countries that may mean lower oil prices and lower profits for the companies that produce the stuff. Take note of news reports concerning companies with shares listed on the stock exchanges, especially those firms whose stock you own or are thinking of buying. But don't let your view of the market outlook change in response to the opinions published each day. If you do, you will never hold your opinion long enough to act on it, and you will become a nervous wreck in the bargain.

Forming your own view of the outlook for the market, and sticking to it until circumstances clearly show you are wrong, is one of the two principal methods of successfully playing the game the self-reliant way. Thriving stock market investors do not hunt with the crowd. They stalk their prizes in lonely isolation, believing that the consensus view of the future is usually wrong — a belief with much evidence to support it. This so-called contrarian view is not as silly as it sounds when you first encounter it. Stock prices rise when there are more people interested in buying than in selling. It should not be surprising, therefore, that the majority of investors are bullish just before the market turns down — and that just before a falling market turns up again, you can hardly find a bullish investor.

The second, and probably easier, approach is to ignore the hullabaloo over what the market is going to do next. Many successful professional and amateur investors do this. Academic evidence suggests there is no connection between what the market did yesterday and what it is likely to do today, next week or next month — the so-called random-walk theory. There is also a lot of historical evidence that suggests it is futile to try to predict how the stock market will react to economic developments in the short term. Traditionally, for instance, it was considered almost a natural phenomenon that investors will react with enthusiasm to an economy that is expanding faster than expected. But at times in the last few years, investors have not always greeted news of faster-than-expected growth with zeal. So even if you had accurately predicted any particular piece of economic good news, you would not necessarily have done well in the stock market by making a short-term investment based on your prediction.

As always, however, some stocks rise and others fall. And frequently the moves are in response to, or in anticipation of, changes in the business fortunes of the companies in question. To follow such news about individual Canadian companies, you must devote

Toronto

Vol (100s)	P/E Yield ratio	52-week high low Stock	Sym	Div	High	Low	Close	Chg	Vol (100s)	P/E Yield ratio	52-week high low Stock
644	4.3 10.8	10.85 6⅞ ♣Rangr Oil	RGO	a0.08	10.25	9.90	10.20	+0.25	3643	1.1 37.1	24¾ 21⅜ Stelco
982	3.5 16.6	15 7.05 Rayrock sv	RAY		7.90	7.90	7.90		17	41.1	21 15.00 ♣Stone-
4	7.4	4.90 4.10 Re'Con Bl	REC		4.80	4.60	4.80	+0.10	78		4.75 2.80 Stressgen
152	2.4 73.1	4.00 2.15 ♣Rea Gold j	REO		2.38	2.25	2.38	+0.13	1844		7½ 4.85 ♣Strong
61		1.50 0.40 Receptagen	RCG		0.63	0.61	0.61	-0.02	186		0.34 0.14 Stroud j n
8	4.7	1.68 0.69 ♣Redaur j	RRK		0.80	0.70	0.74		1096		16 5.00 Summit
1	20.8	3.60 1.59 Redfern j	RFR		2.00	1.95	1.97	-0.03	114		2.90 1.05 Summo N
10255		1.50 0.75 Regional Rs	RGL		1.01	0.98	0.98	-0.04	53	32.7	2.25 0.60 Sun Ice
951	1.0 24.5	4.95 2.40 ♣Reko Intl	REK		4.30	4.30	4.30	-0.20	15	71.7	49.00 39⅛ ♣Suncor
895		7.00 2.25 ♣Remingtn	REL		6.60	6.35	6.60	+0.10	69		10.85 8 Surry Me
26	5.0	40.00 28⅞ Renaissanc	RES		39.65	39.30	39.35	+0.05	2812	37.1 ↑	5.40 2.50 ♣Synerg
918	35.4	7.50 3.55 Repadre Ca	RPD		6.10	6.05	6.10	+0.10	7	38.1 ↑	3.20 2.15 ♣Synsor
11	22.8	10½ 4.85 Repap	RPP		5.45	5.30	5.40		886	36.0	7½ 1.76 ♣Syst X
50	2.3	1.33 0.61 Reserve Ro	ROI		1.24	1.20	1.24	-0.04	348		8.25 3.90 ♣TLC La
9		2.75 1.00 Resourceca	RSC		2.35	2.35	2.35	-0.15	37		10½ 6¼ ♣TSB In
1255	3.1 12.6	3.20 2.00 Revenue	RPC	0.07	2.44	2.44	2.44	+0.04	30	2.9 27.1	3.25 1.40 TVI Pacific
1502	6.3 10.5	10 4.30 Richland	RLP.A		4.45	4.40	4.45	+0.05	167	21.2	15½ 8⅝ ♣TVX Go
30	5.8	5.75 2.75 Richmont Mi	RIC		5.05	5.05	5.05	-0.25	z60	29.7	8.25 6 Taiga Fore
454		14⅜ 11 Rigel Energ	RJL		12.55	12.35	12.40	-0.10	83		35.25 22¾ Talisman
10	17.2	2.70 0.53 Rileys Data	RDI		2.45	2.40	2.45	+0.10	30	9.8	5.00 1.50 Taro
25		28⅞ 23⅜ Rio Algom	ROM	0.70	26.90	26.55	26.85	-0.15	168	2.6 14.4	13.90 10½ ♣Tarrag
10		7.80 3.65 Rio Alto	RAX		7.35	7.30	7.35		61	30.6	10.00 3.00 Tarxien
1210		4.75 2.30 River Gold	RIV		4.15	4.05	4.15	+0.05	85	37.7	3.42 0.60 Tech Flav
111		19¾ 15⅛ Riversid For	RFP	0.24	17.50	17.50	17.50		5	1.4	32.40 23 Teck sv
158		37¾ 27⅞ Rgrs Ca	RCM.B		28.50	28.30	28.40	-0.10	8		2.34 0.54 Tecsyn

SOURCE: THE GLOBE AND MAIL

TABLE III

a little time each day to reading the Report on Business section of Toronto's *Globe and Mail* newspaper. Its large staff keeps a close watch on the Canadian business scene, especially on developments among companies with shares listed on stock exchanges. The paper also tries to keep readers informed about international developments likely to affect Canadian businesses, as does a rival, the daily *Financial Post*, also based in Toronto. For comprehensive coverage of the U.S. business arena, however, you need *The Wall Street Journal*, and for Europe and much of the rest of the world, the *Financial Times* of London, England. You should keep an eye on the business section of your local daily paper for detailed coverage of companies operating in your area, some of which could be rewarding stock market investments.

For the serious stock market player, reading daily newspapers is just a start. Canada has an excellent financial weekly that publishes information and commentary of great help to investors. The weekly edition of *The Financial Post* reports on Canadian and international economic, political and business developments of interest to a wide audience. It provides news and analysis of the stock market as part of this package. All of these publications are available at prices that are bargains if you consider how much of your savings you might lose because you didn't know something they might have told you.

Common to all these publications is a package of daily or weekly stock market quotations. Stock exchanges are fortunate in the fact that newspapers of all sorts devote many columns of space, free of charge, to publishing information on the prices of their products.

The quotation lists vary in the amount of information they contain. At the least, for each stock listed, there is:
- A column usually labelled "stock" for the abbreviated name of the company that issued it,
- A column labelled "high" for the highest price at which the stock traded during the previous day or week,
- A column labelled "low" for the lowest price at which the stock traded during the previous day or week,
- A column labelled "close" or "last" for the price paid in the final normal transaction of the previous day or week,
- A column labelled "change" for the difference between the final price paid on the previous day or week, and the final price of the previous day or week before that,
- A column labelled "vol." or "volume" for the number or volume of shares traded during the previous day or week.

In addition, many publications include columns showing the highest and lowest prices at which a stock traded during the past 52 weeks, the amount of the annual dividend paid by the company, and other information important to investors, such as the dividend yield and the price-earnings ratio which will be explained in Chapter 4.

These information packages also include a selection of indexes and statistical indicators of what is happening in the stock market and the economy. Indexes are the most commonly used measures of market and economic performance. They are calculated in various ways but they all reflect percentage gains or losses in relation to a benchmark figure. They are also usually weighted so a stock selling for a higher price does not, for that reason alone, assume a larger importance in the calculation of the index than a stock selling for a lower price.

The most closely watched indicator of the ups and downs of the Canadian stock market is the 300-stock composite index of the Toronto Stock Exchange, known as the TSE 300. Like all the exchange's basic stock price indexes, it is based on a 1975 value that was set to 1000. The TSE 300 and its various subindexes, introduced at the start of 1977, are the latest and most comprehensive versions of indexes the exchange first began publishing in 1934. Historical figures for the TSE 300 system are available from the beginning of 1956. The main index tracks changes in the market value of a portfolio of 300 representative stocks. It is subdivided into a dozen or so major industrial groups, each containing varying numbers of stocks. These groups are further subdivided into a longer list of subgroups, some of which contain only a few stocks. In May, 1987, the exchange introduced an index that tracks the price changes of only 35 of the most actively traded big-company stocks on its list. In August, 1993, the exchange introduced yet another index that tracks the price changes of 100 of the active stocks on its list, including those in the 35-stock index.

A daily figure for the average price-earnings ratio of all the 300 stocks that make up the composite index is calculated and published by the exchange. This ratio tells you how much investors are paying for each dollar of the total profit earned in the latest 12-month period by the companies whose stocks are included in the index. The higher the ratio, the more expensive the 300 stocks are. You can also compare the ratio for an individual stock with this number to see if investors think the stock is worth more or less than the average market stock. The exchange also calculates and publishes the dividend yield for the index stocks, which is a measure of how much you would get in dividends for each dollar invested in a portfolio consisting of the 300 stocks.

Less well known and not so widely available are the TSE's total return indexes, introduced in 1980. As well as tracking changes in market value caused by the ups and downs in stock prices, these indexes also take dividend payments into account. Calculations for these indexes assume that any dividend payments are reinvested immediately at the current market price. This technique simulates the compound return an investor would receive if he always reinvested the dividend in the stock market. The base for all the total return indexes was set to 1000 at the end of 1976.

The Montreal Exchange beat Toronto to the punch by first publishing market indexes in 1926, eight years ahead of its rival. In those days, Montreal was Canada's principal financial centre, but it has slipped well behind Toronto in recent years and its indexes are not as closely watched. One reason is that, except for particular subgroups from time to time, the movements of Montreal's indexes are similar to those of Toronto. Montreal publishes a Canadian market

The TSE 300 and the Total Return Index January 1981 to July 1996

TSE 300 Composite Index
TSE Total Return Index

SOURCE: TORONTO STOCK EXCHANGE

CHART III

portfolio index composed of 25 high-quality, widely held stocks, plus other group indexes. The Vancouver Stock Exchange also publishes an index designed to track representative price movements of its stocks.

The world's best-known stock market indicator, the Dow Jones industrial average, is made up of just 30 blue-chip U.S. stocks. Yet the movements of this world-famous indicator are what people are usually talking about when they say the U.S. market was up yesterday and holding steady today. Its ups and downs are quoted and thought of as the same thing as the entire New York market, even though around 2,800 stocks of a wide range of differing sorts of companies change hands each day on the New York Stock Exchange. The calculation of the indicator, known familiarly as the Dow, starts similarly to any mathematical average by adding up the prices of the 30 issues. Originally, the price total was then divided by 14, the number of issues in the average when it was launched late last century. But this divisor has been adjusted downward over the years to compensate for stock splits. In mid-1996, it was 0.33792816. There is no weighting to reflect the total number of shares of each company.

A broader set of indexes that are weighted to reflect the total market value of the stocks they include is published by Standard & Poor's Corporation. Its composite index tracks the performance of 500 representative U.S. stocks. The index is subdivided into an industrials index of 400 stocks, a transportation company index of 20 stocks, a financial company index of 40 stocks and a utility company index of 40 stocks. The company also publishes statistics on earnings, dividends, dividend yields and price-earnings ratios related to the index groups. The New York Stock Exchange itself publishes a similar set of indexes, based on a much larger number of stocks. Its composite index includes all common stocks on its list, some 2,000 or so. It is further subdivided into the same four industrial groups, which include all common stocks in each classification.

It is important to be aware that a 52-point drop in the TSE 300 may not amount to the same thing as a 52-point drop in the Dow. With the TSE index at, say, 4000, a slide of 52 points amounts to just 1.3 per cent. If the Dow is at 3000, a slide of 52 points is a change of 1.7 per cent. This is even more important when reacting to changes in the prices of stocks. Again, it's the percentage change that counts. A $1 drop in a $20 stock is 5 per cent, which is not fun but is also not disastrous. If a $100 stock falls by the same amount, the 1 per cent change can even be shrugged off. But if you own a $2 stock that drops by $1, you are down 50 per cent, which most people would consider a serious matter. A clear understanding of basic arithmetic is not essential for doing well in the stock market, but it's a useful asset to help you appreciate what is really happening.

CHAPTER 3

Do You Know Who You Are?

IN HIS 1967 CLASSIC, *THE Money Game,* written under the pseudonym of Adam Smith, George Goodman retold the popular Wall Street story of the professional portfolio manager who consulted a psychiatrist. The expert on markets lay down on the couch and awaited some penetrating questions from the expert on human minds. "Polaroid," said the psychiatrist. "Polaroid," replied the portfolio manager, weighing the possible unconscious implications of this opening. "It's come up awfully fast, hasn't it?" said the psychiatrist. "I have a lot, personally. Do you think I should hold on to it?" The portfolio manager sat up. "It's going to be all right," he said, in soothing tones. "It's going to work out just fine." The psychiatrist slid into a more relaxed position in his chair. "I worry about Polaroid," he confessed. "Let's examine this," said the portfolio manager, "and see why you're so worried. I think I can help."

Psychiatry and the stock market? What's going on here? The market is about solid realities like sales and profits and assets and liabilities, isn't it? You check out the company's business, research its financial statements, calculate the real value of its stock, compare it with the market price, decide whether it's a buy or a sell or something to be avoided entirely, and away you go. Or you chart the movements of prices and the volume of trading, study the patterns to make an educated guess about what's going to happen next, then put your money on the table. No hint of the subconscious there.

Yet here's the rub. If such tangible and fairly easily ascertainable matters were all there was to it, the stock market would be a much less demanding arena in which to play and many more people would be winners. Consider for a moment the sad fact that few brokers make a lot of money from investing in the market. Certainly, many brokers make a lot of money from commissions, and one would think that they, of all people, would be well placed to put that money into good stocks and earn consistent profits. Unlike most people, brokers spend their working hours in close touch with the market. They have first crack at the bright ideas of their firm's expensively trained investment analysts. They can pick up a lot of potentially profitable information from their customers. Yet it's well known in the business that, by and large, brokers lose more often than they win.

The reason is rooted in human psychology. A broker worried about the market may well be recommending the right sort of conservative moves to customers. But the odds are that this same broker is busy buying options, or selling short, or even doubling up on earlier highly leveraged bets. Why? Because that's what's expected of a professional player, by others and by the player himself. Caution, taking the safer option, is for amateurs. I can get away with breaking the rules that apply to others, the expert believes. Let the customer move her money out of the stock market and into the safe harbour of bank term deposits. But that's not for me. There's this nice little stock that hasn't made its move yet, and I can always bail out quickly if things really start falling apart. And so it goes.

A psychiatrist's main tool is encouraging patients to get to know themselves. He or she administers that encouragement in an environment designed to be comfortable and reassuring: the proverbial couch, the calm bedside manner, the persistent but gentle questioning. It can be an expensive business for the patient, of course, but there is this to be said for it: Going to a psychiatrist is usually much cheaper than seeking the same self-knowledge in the stock market, which is what some investors appear to be doing. Goodman's memorable comment sums up the point admirably: "If you don't know who you are, the stock market is an expensive place to find out."

None of this is to say that you have to be mad to venture into the stock market, although sometimes it seems that way. Ironically, it is at just those moments when most people think buying stocks is crazy that the really golden opportunities go begging. What better times were there to buy stocks in the last decade than amid the deep gloom of late 1982, or in November, 1987, just after the October crash?

To understand why stock market investors behave the way they do requires more than a knowledge of facts and numbers. It demands observation of the behaviour of human beings, especially when acting as part of a crowd. It is well known that mob psychology accounts for market panics and market runaways. Less well known is the truth that individual human psychology accounts for much of how investors behave toward the stocks they buy and sell.

Treating the stock like a child or a pet is a common example of what can get you into trouble. It's common to hear a disappointed buyer complain that "the darned thing isn't cooperating" or "what's this stock trying to do to me?" Investors develop love-hate relationships with stocks. When one they buy goes up, they glow like a proud parent at a school concert. When one they buy goes down, they are affronted by such contrary behaviour. Sometimes they even want to teach the stock a lesson by hanging on stubbornly until it behaves better, like training a mischievous puppy.

To say the least, such emotions obscure the issue of whether you should be in the stock in the first place and what to do with it now. You must watch yourself constantly to detect this sort of thing. Once again, Goodman provides a mantra that might help, if chanted softly but regularly each morning the market is open: "The stock doesn't know that you own it." Nor does it care.

The stories brokers tell about their clients, anonymously, of course, contain several common characters. Most notably, there is the client as masochist. This sort of client appears to get a morose kick out of everything the market does to him. He can see the dark cloud behind every silver lining. If a stock he buys goes down, he is not surprised because he figures he deserves to lose. If a stock he buys goes up, he can always point to another one that would have gone up more. Such a client may even do well in the market, but you would never know that from listening to him.

Then there is the client as lonely heart. Buying a stock and putting it away is not for her, even though that frequently works better than busily buying and selling. What this client wants is to be part of the crowd, to keep in touch with the action by calling her broker every other day for a chat about the market, and checking the prices of her stocks in the paper every morning. Advanced cases call every hour and check the quotes on one of the on-line services three or four times a day. Doing well financially does not appear to be the main objective of this sort of client. Making a little or losing a little will be just fine. The most important thing is being up to speed on what's happening.

Then there is the client as passionate believer. Feed him almost any story about a stock and he swallows it happily and places an order. Less scrupulous brokers love this guy. The more scrupulous worry about him. He's happy only when he has a romantic vision about a stock — a vision that frequently survives the most brutal treatment by the market. Like a long-suffering father, he believes that the prodigal son will eventually return home and fulfill all his dreams. Sometimes, he is right; more often, he is wrong.

Different clients need different sorts of psychological triggers to bring them to the point of buying or selling. For many individual customers, it's a good bedside manner that counts. They don't want to hear a lot of facts and statistics, nor are they too interested in hearing bad news. What they want is a reassuring, confident but sympathetic voice on the line, coming from somebody they trust. But others do want the facts and figures, and they would rather hear bad news early enough to have a chance of avoiding trouble. Which kind are you?

Recognizing yourself in one of these portraits could be the best thing that could happen to your stock market career. It could help you avoid money-losing practices you might otherwise stumble into. Learning to know yourself, preferably before venturing into the market, could be very good for your financial health.

CHAPTER 4

Learning the Language

EVERY GAME HAS ITS OWN language. You can't play Monopoly until you are acquainted with such phrases as "passing go," and you won't get very far in hockey without taking the trouble to learn about such matters as "icing." It is the same with more serious forms of endeavour such as making money in the stock market. There is always a jargon that has to be learned and understood.

In the stock market, we have already become familiar with the bulls — those who believe the next move in prices is likely to be up — and their more gloomy cousins, the bears, who believe the next move in prices is likely to be down. Investors can have split personalities: that is, be bullish and bearish simultaneously but selectively. It's possible to believe, for instance, that the market generally is in poor shape but that a particular stock would be a great buy. You can also be enthusiastic about the market as a whole, but be down on a particular stock.

It is said, notably, that bulls can make money and bears can make money, but pigs never make a dime. In other words, allowing greed to get the upper hand has brought many a bull and many a bear to financial disaster. For instance, greed may have the upper hand just when the market or a particular stock reaches a peak. In hindsight, such a moment would be a good time to sell rather than buy. Unfortunately for investors, peaks can usually be recognized only after the fact. You can see them on a chart of prices as the point where an upward trend becomes a downward trend. You can also see their opposite, a trough, or the point where a downward trend changes to an upward trend.

You also probably won't spend too much time reading about professional money managers before encountering the "top-down" and "bottom-up" approaches to investment strategy. The first is a convenient phrase that describes the stock-picking technique of inves-

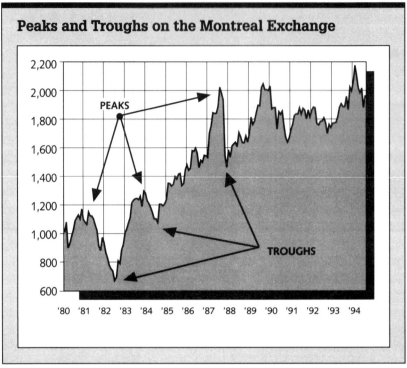

Peaks and Troughs on the Montreal Exchange

CHART IV

tors who first assess the big picture of the economy, then consider the outlook for a particular industry, and only then weigh the performance and prospects of an individual company in that industry. In contrast, practitioners of the "bottom-up" approach go at things the other way around. Their attention is first caught by the circumstances of a particular company. Then, as an aid to making the final investment decision, they will probably cast an eye over the prospects for the particular industry and perhaps even the regional or national economy, although many such players scorn the idea of looking at the big picture.

Knowing the meanings of these two terms is useful but not essential. However, there are some terms and a few basic calculations you must master if you aim to invest seriously. Most notably, you should have a clear understanding of what common stock is and why owning it is potentially more rewarding and riskier than other kinds of stock market investments.

The owners of a company's common stock (also called common shares) are the collective owners of the company. They own what is left after everybody else has taken their piece out of the original sales dollar, including employees, suppliers, creditors and owners of other types of shares. They are in the position of the child who is promised what's left of a favorite treat after the guests have taken their portion. In other words, it could be feast or famine. The capital their shares represent is called the equity capital, and as a result the buying of common shares is sometimes described as buying a piece of the equity. This capital can also be thought of as a shock absorber, expanding when the company does well and compressed when business gets tough.

Preferred shares provide their owners with a fixed dividend that does not usually rise even if the company does well. The dividend is not supposed to fall either, but the company can decide to cut or stop paying preferred dividends at its discretion. The only binding promise the company makes is to pay preferred dividends before it pays common dividends.

It is possible to acquire a claim to the rewards of a common shareholder without putting up the full price of the stock. This can be done by purchasing warrants, rights, receipts or options, rather like putting a down payment on a house. For a smaller amount of money you get the chance to make a big killing if things go well; if they don't, you can lose your entire investment.

You will be aided in playing this tricky game by knowing the differences between blue-chip stocks, penny stocks and the rest of the field. Owning a blue-chip stock, named for the highest value poker chips, makes you part owner of a large, well-established company with many years of business experience under its belt. It is, therefore, unlikely that the stock price will suffer total collapse, but it is equally unlikely that it will double overnight. The stock will normally rise and fall in stately cadence like a big ocean liner and its price will usually be measured in dollars and cents. Owning a penny stock, so named because its price is usually measured in cents only, is more fun because there's a chance it could double or triple in a flash. Its price movements will be more like those of a tiny tramp steamer in a high sea, making it more susceptible to foundering than the blue chip.

Then there are the two most important things, after price, that you should know about any stock you are interested in: its yield and its price-earnings ratio.

The yield, more formally known as the dividend yield, is the annual amount of normal dividend payments as a percentage of the market price. Suppose a company's annual dividend payments add up to $1.60. If the current market price of its stock is $25, the yield will be 6.4 per cent. What this tells you is that for every $1,000 invested in this company's shares at today's price, you can expect to receive $64 in dividends each year. The calculation should not take into account special one-time dividends that companies sometimes pay.

Why is it important to know this? First of all, the calculation tells you what return you will get from your investment if the stock's price remains static. If that happens, and if the company whose shares you bought pays no dividends at all, your return on that particular investment will be a big fat zero. Worse, you will have lost whatever interest you could have earned by putting the money in the bank instead.

Second, the yield figure can be used to compare the returns available on different stocks and even on investments of other types. If the dividend yield on the stock you fancy is just 3 per cent and government bonds offer a 12 per cent return, you had better be sure the stock's price is going to rise and produce a capital gain if you stick with it, even after allowing for the taxman's easier hand on dividends than on bond interest (see Chapter 18).

Dividends are paid out of a company's earnings after all expenses and taxes are provided for. This figure is the fabled "bottom line" of a company's financial statements and it is the key to many things, including the respect of investors. They take a close interest in what portion of earnings would be available for each share if the entire pie were split up. Thus, a company with $1 million of earnings and half a million shares is said to be earning $2 a share.

But that is only part of the story. How much value are investors actually getting when they buy that company's shares on the stock market? The answer is the price-earnings ratio, also known as the stock's multiple. Calculating this is even simpler than calculating the yield; you just divide the market price by the amount of earnings per share. If the shares of our million-dollar company are trading at $20, their price-earnings ratio is 10 (the $20 price, divided by

Price-to-Earnings Ratios

	June 28, 1996	Dec. 31, 1990	Nov. 30, 1987	July 31, 1987
Toronto 35	17.72	12.75	12.79	19.30
TSE 300	19.24	16.09	13.89	21.63
Metals and Minerals	18.74	10.14	23.41	49.96
Gold and Prec. Minerals	71.49	54.63	46.00	52.75
Oil and Gas	30.79	30.88	30.18	NA
Paper and Forest	6.97	31.90	9.84	16.48
Consumer Products	78.20	14.69	11.05	16.39
Industrial Products	17.83	17.30	16.24	28.15
Real Estate & Construction	NA	NA	NA	NA
Transportation/Environ.	25.00	17.16	18.35	22.65
Pipelines	11.43	14.85	14.96	20.13
Utilities	18.55	15.02	10.08	11.01
Communications & Media	28.20	33.00	20.09	26.94
Merchandising	24.63	NA	16.72	17.88
Financial Services	9.29	7.76	7.48	11.02
Conglomerates	NA	15.32	12.48	29.61

Note: The dates July 31, 1987, and Nov. 30, 1987, were chosen to illustrate the dramatic change in price-to-earnings ratios that can occur with a sudden shift in the market, in this instance, the October stock market crash. NA indicates no earnings.

SOURCE: TORONTO STOCK EXCHANGE

TABLE IV

$2 of earnings per share). The price in this calculation is always the current market price, and the ratio you will see included with most published stock quotations is based on actual company earnings during the most recent 12 months. As companies report their earnings to shareholders, at three-month or six-month intervals, the 12-month earnings-per-share figure is updated accordingly. The resulting figure is the "trailing" earnings per share, and the same term is often given to the price-earnings ratio calculated with it.

Investors, however, are usually more interested in what the company is likely to earn next year. What it has already made is history, and investors are not big on past exploits. Their unsentimental approach is to ask what the company is going to do for us tomorrow. Highly paid professional stock analysts spend a lot of time trying to estimate accurately what the companies they follow will earn next year. When your stockbroker tells you enthusiastically that the company whose stock you are considering will earn $1.25 a share this year and $2 next year, almost certainly she will be quoting estimates by the firm's own team of analysts. Check to be sure, however.

A stock's price-earnings ratio is a tool that helps you judge whether it is cheap or expensive. Other things being equal, a $25 stock of a company that will probably earn $1.25 a share is more expensive than a $30 stock of a company that is likely to earn $3 a share — twice as expensive, to be precise, because the first stock has a price-earnings ratio of 20 and the second stock has a ratio of 10.

What makes the stock market tricky, however, is that other things are almost never equal. It may be that the first company has a promising future, with earnings marching upward like a Hollywood-style staircase to the stars. That prospect could easily justify its $25 price. Indeed, if enough investors come to believe in the company's exciting future, a 20-times multiple will appear cheap. Price-earnings ratios of 50 or more are not unknown for the stocks of companies considered to be rising stars. The second company, on the other hand, may be a plodder, a reliable but dull producer of $3 a share, year in and year out. Its 10-times multiple may, therefore, be about right, or perhaps even generous.

Comparisons of a stock's price-earnings ratio with the average multiples for its industry and for the market as a whole are also important. In mid-1996, for instance, the multiple of earnings of the 300 issues that make up the main price-measuring index of the Toronto Stock Exchange was about 19. This index, known as the TSE 300, is designed to reflect the performance of a representative selection of all industry groups with shares listed on the exchange. Among individual groups, however, the multiples varied widely, from 7 to about 80. These differences reflected the varying degrees of investors' enthusiasm for the industries concerned. Within industry groups, there can also be a wide variation between the price-earnings multiples that investors put on individual stocks, even though the companies concerned are in the same kind of business and subject to a similar business environment. The different multiples reflect the market's consensus about such matters as whether each company is improving its financial performance or losing ground, about whether its management is highly regarded, about whether it has a successful takeover record or whether it's likely to be the target of a high-priced takeover bid.

One reason a company could be a takeover target is its "strong" balance sheet. To understand this term we need to take a closer look at the fundamentals of a company's financial statements and consider a few more useful terms and calculations.

Many people have heard of balance sheets. The phrase is used in everyday speech, for example, when someone talks of drawing up a balance sheet of the advantages and disadvantages of doing something. But in the precise sense of the term, a balance sheet is only one of several different tallies of figures that make up a company's financial statements. The most important of the others are the income statement and the cash-flow statement, often called the statement of changes in financial position. While these statements track different aspects of financial performance, they are all linked. Taken together, they keep score of how a company is doing in the business arena.

First, the balance sheet. The most important thing to remember is that it is a snapshot of a company's financial position at a particular time, usually the end of an accounting period such as the firm's financial year. So a balance sheet may be completely accurate today, yet a balance sheet for the same company constructed tomorrow may be quite different but still accurate. A second and better-known fact about balance sheets is that they always balance — the assets on one side and the liabilities on the other side always equal each other. This is not some immutable law of nature; it is merely because of the way balance sheets are constructed. What are the assets and liabilities? Simply and broadly put, a company's assets are what it owns, plus what others owe to it. Its liabilities are what it owes, plus what its shareholders really own but it has the use of — the equity capital of the company.

Included in the assets category are the cash in a company's bank account or in term deposits, its accounts receivable or money owed by its customers for products and services supplied, the plant and equipment it owns, and its inventories of raw materials and products. Conversely, the company's bank loans, its accounts payable (money it owes to suppliers) and its other debts can be clearly seen as liabilities. Curiously, there is usually nothing on a balance sheet to reflect what many people would consider a successful company's greatest asset: the skills and energy of its managers and employees.

In fact, their presence is reflected only as an expense on the income statement. Yet without them, the company might have no value at all. Another major diversion from reality on the balance sheet is that assets and liabilities are almost always recorded at their original cost to the company, and in the case of many assets the figure is reduced each year by an arbitrary amount meant to reflect depreciation in the value of the asset over time. For example, a company's plant will frequently be recorded on the balance sheet at a value much lower than the price the real estate it stands on would fetch in today's market. Awareness of such quirks of business accounting rewarded many investors over the postwar inflationary decades.

Why does the balance sheet always balance? It's because of two key facts:

- Every balance sheet embodies a simple underlying equation: Subtract financial liabilities to others from the company's assets, and what's left belongs to the shareholders;
- What's left of the bottom-line profit or loss on the income statement, after all expenses and dividends to shareholders are paid, is transferred to the balance sheet and increases or reduces the shareholders' piece of the pie after accounting for liabilities.

The income statement is the second of the three major financial statements produced by a company for its shareholders, and probably the easiest to understand. It is a summary of the company's sales or business revenue over a period of time, less expenses of all kinds. The difference between the two, before any dividend payments to shareholders, represents the company's net profit or loss. Companies rarely pay out all of their profits to shareholders, preferring to retain some, and frequently all, to be reinvested in the business. The amount not paid out shows up on the balance sheet, usually under the heading of retained earnings, and is counted as part of the shareholders' equity.

Unlike the snapshot provided by a balance sheet, an income statement provides a report on progress over time. It supplies part of the historical link between a balance sheet constructed on, say, the last day of the company's financial year and a balance sheet constructed on the last day of the previous financial year, 12 months earlier. But it doesn't supply the complete picture, partly because it records only money flowing in or out of the company in the normal course of business. Money the company borrows to finance its operations or to expand is not counted as part of its sales or revenue, although the interest paid is counted as an expense and shown on the income statement. Similarly, money spent to make a capital investment such as a plant expansion is not counted as an expense on the income statement, although the additional sales of products made in the expanded plant will be counted when they are made.

The missing portion of the historical link is supplied by the cash-flow statement. As its name implies, this is a summary of all the cash that flows into the company over a period of time from whatever source, less all the cash that flows out for whatever purpose. If a company is established and doing well, this statement is normally of lesser importance. But the signals it gives of impending financial trouble can frequently be spotted by alert investors well before the signs show up on the income statement and the balance sheet. A company can, for instance, appear to be doing very well by making lots of additional sales of a great product, but if it cannot lay hands on sufficient cash to keep its employees paid and its suppliers and creditors happy, it may go out of business. Such unpleasant surprises make bankers grey before their time and smart investors wary.

CHAPTER 5

Meet Your Broker

THERE ARE ROUGHLY 25,000 people in Canada entitled to call themselves investment brokers, and when the market is running strong it seems that everybody knows a good one. Let the market go into a slump, though, and yesterday's heroes and heroines become today's villains. Few emotions are stronger than those inspired by having lost money in the market, and it's almost always possible to blame your broker. Who was it who took your money and put it into that sure thing, anyway?

Dealing with a broker is inescapable, though, if you're going to engage in some do-it-yourself stock market investing. They have a monopoly on the business. You can't take out an advertisement in the local paper or put up a sign and expect to find other investors flocking to pay you the market price for those shares you got through the company's stock-purchase plan. It's probably not legal, anyway, without a licence.

In return for a commission or a quarterly fee a broker, now often called an investment adviser, will endeavour to sell your shares at the best available current price, or at a price that you designate. A broker will also, for a similar commission or fee, endeavour to buy the shares you want at the lowest available price, or at a price you set. A broker will also advise you whether it seems like a good idea to sell or buy. But remember, unless you make a transaction or agree to pay the quarterly fee, the broker gets nothing, just like any other salesman. The fact is that the person you deal with at a brokerage firm, officially known as a registered representative, is merely a superior sort of salesman. He or she will be better educated and spin a fancier and more complicated tale than your average door-to-door peddler of encyclopedias, but the economic basics are the same. No order or fee, no pay!

There is nothing odd about this. Salesmen are the combat soldiers of the business world and nothing is achieved without them.

No business is done until somebody buys something, whether it's a $200 vacuum cleaner, $5,000 worth of shares or a multibillion-dollar supersonic jet. Like many salesmen, however, brokers have difficulty getting respect, which is probably why the official literature of their trade abounds with high-sounding phrases. Take this paragraph from the *Manual for Registered Representatives* for example: "Your position requires absolute trustworthiness; a desire to assist your clients in attaining their investment objectives; a knowledge of individual securities, industries and business conditions; a thorough understanding of the rules of regulatory bodies and absolute observance of these rules; and loyalty to your firm and care for its financial and ethical responsibilities."

No doubt many registered representatives make a valiant effort to live up to these standards, but few can be expected to be the paragons of business virtue described by the manual's publishers, the Canadian Securities Institute. The institute is the national educational organization supported by Canada's five stock exchanges and the Investment Dealers Association of Canada, the brokers' trade group.

As with any supplier of personal services, the best way to find a broker is by word-of-mouth recommendation. Ask your friends and relatives for somebody who has personal experience, but be wary of fond mothers trying to steer business to their inexperienced offspring. Remember that you can't just go by the reputation of the employer; the relationship between commission salesmen such as brokers and the firm where they work is more like that of an independent contractor than an employee. Dealing with a big, established firm will probably ensure reasonable standards of honesty and a minimum level of competence, but that minimum can be surprisingly low, especially at times when a roaring bull market has brought a stampede of newcomers to the business. You can find a good broker at big firms and small firms, at long-established outfits and at hot new ventures. And inevitably you can find bad ones at all of these.

A bit of good luck helps. If you aren't aware of anybody who has ever dealt with a broker, you may end up picking a firm out of the telephone book. That can work out well, too, if you ask for the branch manager. Otherwise you'll be put in touch with the duty broker assigned to answer cold calls from potential new customers, who may not always be somebody you should give your business to.

New Account Application Form

BUSINESS PHONE	HOME PHONE	DATE	ACCOUNT NUMBER	F.A

SURNAME MR. MRS. MS MISS	GIVEN NAMES	SOCIAL INSURANCE NO.

ADDRESS	
CITY	CLIENT CITIZENSHIP

PROVINCE	POSTAL CODE	

SPECIAL INSTRUCTIONS	ACCOUNT TYPE		LANGUAGE	CURRENCY
☐ TSF TO STREET FORM AND HOLD	☐ CASH	☐ MARGIN	☐ ENGLISH	☐ CANADIAN
☐ TSF TO CLIENT'S NAME AND DELIVER	☐ RRSP	☐ QSSP		
	(ATTACH AGREEMENT)	☐ ACCESS	☐ FRENCH	☐ U.S. FUNDS
	(ATTACH AGREEMENT)	(ATTACH AGREEMENT)		
	☐ DAP	☐ DISCRETIONARY		
	☐ MANAGED	☐ RRIF (ATTACH AGREEMENT)		

DAP ☐ DUPLICATE CONFIRMATION ☐ AND/OR STATEMENT ☐ TO:

NAME			
ADDRESS	CITY	PROV.	POSTAL CODE

EMPLOYER'S NAME	EMPLOYER'S ADDRESS
TYPE OF BUSINESS	POSITION	BIRTHDATE

SPOUSE'S NAME	SPOUSE'S EMPLOYER	SPOUSE'S OCCUPATION	SPOUSE'S INCOME

INVESTMENT KNOWLEDGE	FAMILY STATUS	ANNUAL INCOME	NET WORTH
☐ EXCELLENT	☐ SINGLE	LESS THAN $25,000 ☐	LESS THAN $50,000 ☐
☐ GOOD	☐ MARRIED	$25,000 - $50,000 ☐	$50,000 - $100,000 ☐
☐ FAIR	☐ WIDOWED	$50,000 - $100,000 ☐	$100,000 - $200,000 ☐
☐ POOR	☐ DIVORCED	$100,000 - $150,000 ☐	$200,000 - $500,000 ☐
	☐ DEPENDENTS _____	OVER $150,000 ☐	OVER $500,000 ☐

PAST EXPERIENCE		INVESTMENT OBJECTIVES		RRSP/RRIF	APPROXIMATE AMOUNT OF
☐ STOCKS	☐ BONDS	INCOME	%	%	CAPITAL AVAILABLE FOR
☐ SHORT SALES	☐ OPTIONS	LONG-TERM GROWTH	%	%	INVESTMENT
☐ COMMODITIES	☐ OTHERS	SHORT-TERM TRADING	%	%	
☐ MUTUAL FUNDS	☐ NONE	SPECULATIVE	%	%	
Size of ACCT. $ _____		OTHER (EXPLAIN)	%	%	$ _____

HOW LONG HAVE YOU KNOWN THE CLIENT? _____

☐ PHONE-IN ☐ WALK-IN ☐ PERSONAL CONTACT ☐ ADVERTISING LEAD

REFERRAL BY _____

INITIAL ORDER	INITIAL DEPOSIT	☐ BUY ☐ SELL
		☐ SOLICITED ☐ UNSOLICITED

CREDIT REFERENCE

BANK NAME _____   BRANCH _____

ACCT # _____   INFORMATION VERIFIED? ☐ YES ☐ NO

DOES THE CLIENT HAVE RELATED ACCOUNTS AT MW?	ACCOUNTS WITH OTHER FIRMS
☐ NO ☐ YES # _____	☐ NO ☐ YES NAME _____

NAMES OF PUBLIC COMPANIES WHICH CLIENT IS OFFICER OR DIRECTOR	NAMES OF PUBLIC COMPANIES WHICH CUSTOMER OWNS/CONTROLS 10% OR MORE OF VOTING RIGHTS
☐ NONE ☐ _____	☐ NONE ☐ _____

Does anyone other than the persons named have authority over or any financial interest in the account?   ☐ Yes ☐ No
Is the Client a Corporation, Trust, Partnership, etc ?   ☐ Yes ☐ No   If Yes to any of these attach necessary documentation

F.A. is permitted to trade only with clients who are resident in the Province in which he is registered, except in the case of family members, in which case the relationship must be stated _____

THIS INFORMATION IS FULL AND COMPLETE AND MIDLAND WALWYN MAY RELY THEREON UNTIL THE UNDERSIGNED SENDS WRITTEN NOTICE OF ANY SIGNIFICANT CHANGES.

DATED _____   SIGNED _____

WITNESS _____   SIGNED _____

THE UNDERSIGNED REQUESTS THAT A MARGIN ACCOUNT BE OPENED AND AGREES TO THE TERMS OF THE MARGIN AGREEMENT ON THE REVERSE SIDE. IT IS ALSO UNDERSTOOD THAT A MARGIN ACCOUNT INVOLVES THE BORROWING OF MONEY FOR ACCOUNT TRANSACTIONS.

SIGNED _____
(ONLY IF MARGIN ACCOUNT REQUESTED)

REPRINTED BY PERMISSION OF MIDLAND WALWYN INC.

TABLE V

Determine how big the firm is. How many brokers does it have? How many offices? Is it an international giant, a big national Canadian firm or a small regional or local outfit? A big firm will have more and better-qualified people on staff to come up with investment ideas, but you are unlikely to have much personal contact with them. The big firm will also have more new issues of company stock to sell, but it may also be more reluctant to be critical of the investment merits of the companies that are the source of such business. Depending on your tastes, you may be more comfortable with a small firm where you could become almost part of the family and where more independent advice may be obtained although its limited resources could cramp your style now and then.

Almost certainly, your search will not end with the first broker to whom you give an order for shares. A period of trial and error is inevitable. You may discover quickly that you just can't get along with the broker that your best friend swears by. It may be a question of style or chemistry. Whatever the problem, don't tough it out. Pay what you owe, bid a polite goodbye and continue your search. The working relationship between a serious do-it-yourself investor and the broker who supplies advice and executes the orders should feel good. It is very personal and crucially important, so you may work your way through a long list of brokers before finding the ideal partner.

Your newly met broker will have some things on his or her mind, too. First, there is some information that a stockbroker is required by stock exchange and government regulations to obtain from you, under the "know-your-client" rule. In addition to questions about your name, address, telephone number and social insurance number, you will be asked what you know about investing, how much you make, what assets you own and how much you owe. You will also be asked about your investment objectives, and you will have to say just a little more than "to make a lot of money in a hurry." You will be asked, for example, whether you want to put safety ahead of everything, or whether you are prepared to take some risks to make your capital grow more quickly.

If it sounds like the process is similar to applying for credit, that's no coincidence. It is. One of the aims of the exercise is to enable your broker to know enough about you to steer you toward investments that you understand and which are suitable to your financial condition, and to direct you away from unsuitable gambles on which you can't afford the risk. That doesn't mean your broker will necessarily do either of those things, although a good one will.

There is a second aim to the get-acquainted process. Brokers, like other business people, want to get paid. The nature of their business means they take considerable credit risks with their customers. The stock market, with all its failings and dishonesties, still is based on an admirable principle: My word is my bond. Large amounts of money are committed by the players on nothing more than a telephone call, a fax or a message on a computer terminal, and settlement of a transaction frequently does not occur for several days. When you call your broker with an order for some shares while the market is open, one of the firm's traders will buy them for you at the going price, committing the firm to pay that price to some other firm a few days later. You usually don't have to send a cheque or bring in cash first.

Normally, there's no problem. The customer pays as agreed, and all along the line everybody gets paid. But a lot can happen, even in a day or two. Until mid-1995, the normal settlement period for customers was five working days. It's now three business days for most transactions. On just one day in October, 1987, some $37 billion was sliced off the value of stocks listed on the Toronto exchange. In one trading session in June, 1993, when the stock market was doing pretty well, the price of Northern Telecom shares plunged $10, dropping from $47 to $37, and went lower still in four successive sessions. Now suppose you had placed an order to buy some at $47. By the time you were to pay for the shares, they were worth 25 per cent less than you thought. Might you have been tempted to renege on the deal? Well, maybe you wouldn't, but it does happen now and then. Ask any broker. True enough, the firm still has the shares to sell. But the fall in the market price means it will take a loss. And the rules of the game put the broker who took the order on the hook for at least part of that loss. So while your new financial partner is asking you all those questions for the file, he or she is trying also to decide whether you are likely to turn out to be a deadbeat. If there is some doubt, the firm can, and often will, call for a credit check, just like your bank may do if you apply for a loan.

Assuming you pass that inspection and you start dealing with the broker you have found, how do you judge whether you've landed a good one? Here are some rules of thumb:

- First, there is the question of personal chemistry. You alone have to be the judge of that.
- Second, there is the acid test of whether it turns out to be a profitable relationship for both of you. By and large, taking the bad with the good and allowing for all the circumstances, such as your own misguided obstinacy, are you making any money from the market? Is your broker getting enough financial return to stay interested?
- Third, does he or she listen to what you say you want and come up with interesting ideas along those lines, or are you dealing with the kind of broker who calls you indiscriminately to peddle whatever the firm is pushing this week? Are the ideas based on accurate information and solid reasoning? You can't demand a perfect record, but is the broker more often right than wrong?
- Fourth, does your broker take an interest in your overall financial condition, advising you how much of your assets you should put in the stock market and how much you should keep in safer spots? Does your broker from time to time suggest that the market is no place for any of your assets and advise you to wait for a time when there will be better bargains? If so, you may have found a jewel.

A lot depends on the sort of customer you are. The ideal customer, from the broker's point of view, is one who trades frequently, seldom calls just to chat and always pays on time. If you are the kind who calls every day to check prices and chat about the market, and has to be reminded several times to send in the cheque, you had better trade often in order to make it worthwhile for your broker to pay attention. As usual in business relationships, mutual respect and politeness produce the best service. If your broker behaves in a way that doesn't earn your respect, move on and find one who does win it.

Problems, sometimes costly ones, commonly arise over the different kinds of orders you can give your broker. Often, you will give your broker an order to buy or sell a certain number of shares "at the market." This means buy the shares at the lowest possible price or sell them at the highest price available. Among other kinds are:

- Limit order: You set a specific price for the transaction. If the trader can't get that price, the order is not to be executed. If the trader can get a better price, however, the transaction should go through.

Comparing Brokers' Commissions

	Value of order	Typical full commission	Typical discount commission
100 shares at $15	$1,500	$75	$30 – $45
200 shares at $30	6,000	150	35 – 47
500 shares at $20	10,000	235	45 – 60

TABLE VI

• Day order: This order is good only for the day on which it is given. All orders are considered to be in this category unless you specify otherwise. Day orders may be at the market or subject to other specified restrictions.

• Open, or good-until-cancelled, order: This is also known as a GTC. You tell your broker to keep trying to execute this order until you cancel it. This is usually a limit order at a particular price, and it provides particularly fertile ground for misunderstandings. Good brokers will remind their customers of outstanding open orders, particularly during vacation season. But it is always up to you to cancel an open order if you no longer want it to be executed. Many a nasty surprise has happened to customers who forgot about one.

These are the kinds of orders you will mostly use, but there are other more complicated varieties which are used mostly by professional investors and traders.

Of course, if you think your broker is behaving dishonestly or doing things without your approval, you can complain all the way up the line. The conduct of brokers is tightly regulated and few firms relish the potential bad publicity an angry client can inspire. Your first move if things have reached this serious stage should be to seek an appointment with your broker's branch manager. Most problems get straightened out at that stage, but if you still aren't satisfied, you can take your complaint to the local office of the Investment Dealers Association of Canada or to the stock exchange where the transaction took place or where the firm is a member.

All these bodies have powers to investigate and discipline brokers under their jurisdiction. If things have got to this stage, always make your complaint in writing and back it up with the relevant documents. Oral complaints don't get very far. As a last resort, you can go to provincial government securities regulators. Normally, if you go there first, you will be referred back down the line.

There is a new and more subtle aspect to the relationship between brokers and clients that needs to be closely watched. Traditionally in Canada, brokerage firms were owned by their employees. Although there were usually close business relationships with other financial service organizations such as banks, trust companies and the like, there remained a considerable degree of independence for the firms. If they decided to peddle a stock of questionable investment merit to unsuspecting clients, they did it because it was their own idea, not because a parent company told them to. Today, though, many brokerage firms are owned by banks, trust companies and other financial-service groups, all with business and investment interests of their own which may or may not coincide with the best interests of their brokerage subsidiary's clients. The better parent groups are well aware of the suspicions of some clients and have tried to set up procedures to handle potential conflicts of interest. However, it remains to be seen how well these will work, and there are always those outfits that don't bother with such niceties. There are reports of moves to stifle critical public comments by a firm's investment analysts on stocks of companies that are customers of a parent firm.

So what is an investor to do? Clearly, it's necessary to be alert to the possible problem if the brokerage firm you are dealing with does belong to a corporate group with many other interests. Equally clearly, this situation is yet another reason for making the effort to go the do-it-yourself route. Doing so will mean you will not be totally dependent on investment ideas from the firm, which certainly may be based on good research but may occasionally also stem from undisclosed corporate interests.

One other solution is to do without advice from a full-service broker and choose from what are known as discount brokerage firms. Considering the poor quality of the advice given by some brokers, this might save you money even if you still had to pay the normal commission rate. However, there is the additional benefit of a big break on the commission, as much as an 85 per cent discount. Typically, you would pay around $200 commission at a full-service firm on a $10,000 transaction involving 500 shares at $20 apiece, or a charge of 2 per cent. A discounter would probably charge you about $60, or 0.6 per cent, on the same transaction. However, for very small transactions, there is not that much difference. Discounters and full-service firms usually charge flat-rate minimum commissions ranging from $25 to $85. In addition, frequent traders in substantial amounts of stock can negotiate big reductions in commissions even at a full-service firm.

One big bank, The Toronto-Dominion, chose to get into the brokerage business by setting up its own discount-brokerage business instead of buying an established full-service firm, like its rivals did. The experience has not been too rewarding for the bank, however. Dealing with discount brokers has never caught on as much as you might expect. The share of the Canadian market won by the discounters is still only about 20 per cent. Even in the U.S., where investors tend to go at such things more enthusiastically, the discounters' market share is only about 33 per cent.

There is a reason for this. Few investors like to play the market alone. The majority prefer the feeling of being in on the action that they get from calling their broker and talking about what's going on. They, and probably you, need the support and comfort a good broker can give. The stock market's vagaries have humbled the most self-confident of players, and for many people the humiliation is easier to bear in company than alone.

CHAPTER 6

Meet the Analysts

IT PROBABLY WASN'T LONG after you started reading or listening to stock market commentaries that you encountered the analysts, known more precisely as investment analysts or market analysts. Like ancient soothsayers, they are consulted frequently by journalists seeking to enlighten their audience on the latest developments in the world of business and finance. Did the market drop yesterday? Analysts will tell us why. A takeover bid was launched? Check with analysts for opinions on whether the bidder is offering an attractive price. Changes in the corporate tax rules? Find analysts who can say what the impact will be on the bottom line in various industries. Did the budget go far enough in trimming the government's financial deficit? Analysts will provide a hardheaded assessment to put the politicians' promises in perspective. Where are interest rates heading? No problem. We'll round up some analysts for expert opinions.

But who are these analysts? Surely they aren't the same ones immortalized in the classic screen line: "Now just lie back on the couch and tell me all about your problem." No, indeed, although some of the more poetic market analysts in full flight are reminiscent of a psychoanalyst or two seen in 1950s movies. What, after all, are we to make of such comments as: "The market is tired and needs some time to recuperate before trying for new highs"? Some embittered investors may also feel that a psychoanalyst could do as well as anyone at predicting where the stock market is headed.

Investment analysts are employed by full-service brokerage firms and other professional market players such as mutual fund and pension fund managers to seek out profitable opportunities and to explain them to clients. Unlike the brokerage firms' sales representatives, they do not live or die by earning commissions or fees. They are paid a salary — good by most standards but not usually all that good by investment industry measures. Don't weep for them, though. If they are any good at all, they earn big bonuses, which are based on a share of the income their efforts help bring the firm. This arrangement is designed to give analysts the time and incentive to do some thinking. The idea is to insulate them a bit from the daily toil and struggle faced by sales representatives. Never forget, though, when dealing with any investment industry professional, that the industry lives on sales ability. Successful analysts are almost always good at persuading the customers to buy or sell. The most brilliant research idea in the world does not mean much in the investment business unless it is sold effectively.

Unless you are a million-dollar-plus investor, it's unlikely you will have an individual relationship with an investment analyst. You will see their names on the research material your broker gives you to back up a recommendation or merely to impress you with the brains the firm has operating behind the scenes. You will see the better-known or more publicity-hungry analysts quoted in newspapers and magazines, or on radio or television programs. But for the most part, expensive analysts spend their time wooing professional managers of the multibillion-dollar pools of money in pension funds and in financial companies of all kinds. It can take as much time and effort to win a $5,000 stock order from you as it takes to win a $500,000 order from a mutual fund manager. On which would you concentrate?

This does not mean analysts are of little consequence to your do-it-yourself career in the stock market. It is their thinking, their assessment of ever-changing circumstances, that filters through the market to become the conventional wisdom of the day about what's going on and what's likely to happen. You may not agree with this generally accepted picture, but it's important for you to know what it is. Even if your plan is to bet against it — by selling stocks you believe are expensive, to people who believe they are cheap, for instance — you should be aware of why the crowd is thinking that way.

A large brokerage firm may spend a lot of money and have as many as two dozen analysts on staff, each with a different area of research to follow but united in the quest for money-making ideas that they and the firm's salesmen can pitch to customers. A small firm may have two or three, or frequently none at all. But it may buy off-the-shelf research material from firms that specialize in that business. Often, the material will be sent out or given to clients on the smaller firm's letterhead, even if its own staff has had nothing to do with preparing it. It's a cheap way of providing a research service, but that does not mean the advice will necessarily be bad. You can't judge investment research by its packaging or by the number of experts involved in preparing it.

Analysts employed by the brokerage firms come in two basic varieties, divided according to the approach they take to predictions. There are the "fundamental" analysts who research what is going on in the economy, in the industries they watch and in the companies they follow. They keep an eye on such things as the unemployment rate, interest rates, store sales, developments in technology, corporate strategies, balance sheets, acquisition successes and failures, and management's record of achievement or disaster. All of these are carefully scrutinized for an impact on the bottom line. In other words, these analysts study the fundamentals of what makes an economy, an industry or a company tick. Then they use what they have learned to forecast the future performance of companies whose stocks they follow, and in some cases of the stock market in general.

Some fundamental analysts do most of their research in the seclusion of their office, poring over statistics and information in search of the truth. These isolationists stay away from management personnel for fear their judgments will be distorted by contact with people whose job involves being a cheerleader. They place great emphasis on facts and figures, and less reliance on personal intuition. Others believe it is important to mingle with the folks on the corporate firing line. This type of analyst will contentedly sit through a company president's dull luncheon speech, loaded with propaganda and wishful thinking, in return for an opportunity to quiz the great man and his aides afterwards. They will wine and dine industry experts, build relationships with rising corporate stars, play the contacts game with verve and enthusiasm in search of enlightening information that leads to investment profits, while usually stopping short of breaking insider-trading rules.

The other variety are called "technical" analysts. They believe studying fundamentals is a waste of time and energy because, in their opinion, no one has yet established a reliably scientific method of predicting a company's future performance from its past. Instead, they prefer to study price movements of individual stocks and various mathematical indicators that track the movements of groups of stocks and the market as a whole. Operating like physicians studying body-temperature readings and pulse counts, they believe they don't have to look further than the patient's vital signs to make a diagnosis, then a prognosis. Technical analysts argue that the things studied by fundamental analysts are dangerous distractions, more likely to confuse than enlighten. For them, the truth about the future can be divined in the collective wisdom of the market as reflected in stock prices.

It may seem that this sort of analyst is frequently more helpful with the diagnosis than the prognosis. It is easier to explain in hindsight why the market began the year with a brisk rise, followed by a sickening slide and subsequent upward meandering, than it is to predict what will happen next. Things are not made easier by the jargon of technical analysts. Here, for instance, is a leading Canadian technical analyst on his favourite subject, the price of gold: "We've had three distinct waves down in gold since late 1987, and a lot of divergences have been shaping up since September 1988 which lead (and have previously) to my speculation that the bottom may have been made. More confirmations will be necessary, and $395 on the upside must be taken out, but that could come pretty quickly." Does this mean it's time to invest in gold or the shares of gold-producing companies? It's hard to say. What this analyst seems to be saying is that a rise in the price of gold is long overdue, but he doesn't know when it is coming. His predictions are so well hedged, though, that he wins either way. If gold keeps going down, he can claim he didn't say its next move was up. But if it turns around and heads upward, he can say later that he told the customers so. Meanwhile, those customers would be hard pressed to know what to do right now.

Technical analysis does rest on some acute perceptions of human behaviour, though. Even a cursory glance at the price charts that are the principal visual tool of such analysts will show you repetitive patterns of movement, especially when the volume of shares traded is plotted in conjunction with the price.

Consider, for example, a typical experience of an investor who, with mixed fear and anticipation, has laid out a bundle of money to buy a stock for the first time. Checking the price each day, the poor fellow finds that it is going down fast, not rising as his hot tip predicted. The smart thing at that point would probably be to admit to a mistake, cash in the remaining chips and look for another stock. Hardly anybody does that, though; early defeat is hard to take. What

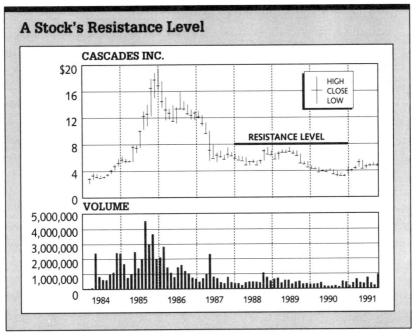

A Stock's Resistance Level

CHART V

usually happens is that the suffering investor sits paralyzed, promising himself that the stock is going to come back. And if it does? At that point he bestirs himself, sells the stock and gets out at the break-even point.

If a lot of investors bought the stock on the same hot tip, a chart of the price movements and trading volume will almost certainly show a familiar pattern. There will be a flurry of trading at the original price, followed by a fall-off in trading as the stock first drops, then recovers toward the original price. Another flurry of trading will take place when the stock nears the original price as the thankful recipients of the not-so-hot tip take their money out. This can happen a number of times, producing an oscillating pattern of prices. A technical analyst who had noted the pattern would identify the original price as a resistance level where an upward price movement is likely to stall. She would also draw conclusions about future price movements if the stock suddenly breaks through that point without first delaying there.

The problem of understanding what an analyst is really telling you is not restricted to the technical variety. Fundamental analysts can be just as opaque. Take this example from a report produced by the research department of a Canadian brokerage house: "While we continue to view [this company] as an insurance company of the highest quality, the operating environment may prove to be a little more challenging over the next 18 months . . . . Thus, limited short-term stock price appreciation may ensue." This extract was part of the firm's explanation of a change in its recommendation on the stock to a "hold" from a "buy." Roughly translated, it appears to mean that the firm's analyst was not sure the company's management could handle what was seen to be coming down the pike, a conclusion that might lead a wary investor to sell rather than sit tight.

In part, these communications problems result from the use of jargon, a handy shorthand for experts talking to each other, but not helpful in communicating with outsiders. There is another reason, though. It has to do with the need to wrap up unpalatable truths in bland packaging.

Most everybody is happy with the analyst who recommends a stock as a good buy. The company's management sees virtue rewarded, clients get excited at the prospect of making a profit, and sales representatives are elated by the thought of the commissions they will earn when clients climb aboard. In contrast, the analyst who recommends selling a stock finds it a lonely business. The company's management will be angry. The boss may be angry if the company has pull with the brokerage firm's top brass. Even clients, in whose interest the analyst made the call, will for the most part not be happy. Some of those who already own the stock may act on the sell recommendation, but most probably won't. People don't like admitting to a mistake, which is what selling a losing stock amounts to. Clients who don't own it won't do anything either, except the small minority who may sell it short (see Chapter 14). So the sales representatives are unhappy, too, because of lost commissions.

So how is the pessimistic analyst to retain some self-respect? The answer, frequently, is to use code phrases in the recommendation. Another technique is to use a numbered rating system: 5 for "rush out and buy this stock now," 1 for "don't go near this disaster." The bad news doesn't sound so grim when presented as a number.

These methods convey a clear enough message to the initiated. Their use also provides an alibi if a client later asks the firm why its high-priced analysts didn't spot a loser. Such wrapped-up warnings are given surprisingly often. The trouble is that uninitiated clients may not recognize them. To help you do so, here is a selection of commonly used euphemisms, with irreverent translations:

• "This stock is suitable for the patient, long-term investor."
Translation: Buy this only if you can wait a lifetime and, even then, don't count on it.

• "Management of this company has ambitious plans for future growth."
Translation: We didn't say their plans make any sense.

• "This company's financial performance will continue to deteriorate. The emphasis on stock price performance will shift from an earnings play to an asset play. Superior stock price performance is only likely to be achieved with an asset restructuring which seeks to maximize shareholder's value. Otherwise, the stock will underperform the market over the next 12 months."
Translation: While we didn't actually say sell this loser, realistically the only hope for it is the unlikely possibility that the company's management can come up with some kind of gimmick that gets investors excited about it again.

• "In our opinion the stock cannot be the star performer it used to be and it follows that it must now be evaluated by different parameters."
Translation: Hold on to this if you really must, but don't say we didn't warn you.

• "In view of the stock's defensive characteristics . . . a degree of overvaluation could be expected, but at $24 and upwards a gradual reduction in positions is recommended."
Translation: There are always fools out there who will pay too much for a stock but it's a good idea not to be one of them.

You will almost certainly encounter early in your stock market career a special sort of analyst who does not work for brokerage firms or for the professional managers of pension funds or mutual funds. Most of these people are not shy about recommending what you should buy and what you should sell. They are the authors of the 1,000 or so market letters published in North America, a diverse bunch ranging from holders of Ph.D. degrees in economics and finance to at least one former night club singer and one rock guitarist. What they have in common is that they all offer, explicitly or implicitly, what everyone would like to find: a no-sweat method of making big money from the stock market in return for an annual subscription fee ranging from $50 to $500 or more.

If they delivered consistently on that alluring promise, their fees would seem modest. But they don't. One of the few things that can be said with certainty about the stock market is that there is no easy way of consistently doing well, in other words beating the market's average performance. It is extremely difficult to do, which is a good reason for staying clear of anybody who claims to make spectacular profits all the time. Yet a second thing that can be said with reasonable confidence is that it is not impossible. So while most market-letter authors do not consistently deliver better than average recommendations, a handful do, at least for a while.

Unfortunately, research on the success of these authors is murky, for two reasons. First, because there is so much money riding on the answers, it's very difficult to get unbiased evidence. Second, the small group of academics who study these matters battle each other with mathematical weapons that most market players, and almost everybody else, do not understand. Their battle is over something called the efficient-market hypothesis, also known as the random-walk theory. If correct, this theory undermines the foundations of the entire investment business. Simply put, it says that all relevant information will be immediately reflected in the current price of a stock the moment that it becomes available. In addition, it says that the previous history of a stock's price provides no useful information about what the price will do next. In other words, stock prices always vary in a random way around a pretty accurate valuation. The implication is that investment research of any variety is a waste of time, effort and money. Stock pickers stay in business only because of dumb luck.

In the 1970s, the random-walk advocates were riding high, but in the past decade their opponents have gained ground. Evidence has mounted that the stock market is nowhere near as efficient as once thought. New information is not available to every player at the same time. What's more, investors do not react immediately and in similar fashion to information when they receive it. Everyone does not have the same ability to make accurate forecasts and correct decisions. As a result, so-called market anomalies continue to plague the lives of the random-walkers. More reliable information has become available about the records of a handful of professional money managers who consistently beat the market over long periods of time, presumably by exploiting such market anomalies. In short, it seems that it might be possible, after all, for a few authors of market letters to do the same thing.

Still, you should remain wary of market-letter analysts. The danger is not in wasting the subscription money; it lies in following the author's recommendations about where to risk large amounts of your savings. The safest rule is that the more alluring and glittering the sales pitch, the less interested you should be. Words such as "easy" or "quick" are unmistakable warning signals. This does not mean you can't lose money by acting on the recommendations made in a market letter that is sold almost apologetically and looks like a computer printout. It's just that you're more likely to be trusting and uncritical when your head is filled with the easy-money dreams spun by a skilled advertising copywriter.

Stay away from market letters that haven't been around for at least 10 years. A decade is usually long enough for the authors to have been through at least one bad bear market and to have learned something from the experience. Like the entire investment business, market letters flourish luxuriantly in bull markets but a serious downturn always kills off much of the new crop. The survivors are scarred but usually smarter.

Some market letters provide more than market advice. They may contain literate commentaries on the vagaries of the financial markets, the economy and the state of the world in general. They may provide articulate statements of opinions you agree with. Investors frequently subscribe to letters for that reason alone. Believers in gold buy letters that blame the world's ills on the adoption of paper currency. People excited by fast-paced stock trading buy letters that have lots of buy and sell recommendations in each issue. People who get their kicks from poring over charts and statistics buy letters that are full of them. If you find a letter that is worth its subscription for such a reason, go ahead and subscribe. If you enjoy reading it, the subscription will be worth the money. Just don't let its author take complete charge of your investments.

CHAPTER 7

Getting the Rhythm

IF YOU HAD BOUGHT A representative group of stocks at the market's high point in August, 1987, just before the big crash in October of that year, it would have taken you nearly two years to break even on the investment, including dividend payments. If you had done the same thing just before the great crash of 1929, it would have taken more than 15 years to break even. These striking figures from analyst Laurence Siegel of Chicago-based Ibbotson Associates, quoted in a *Wall Street Journal* story, suggest strongly that good timing is an important ingredient in successful stock market investing. They are based on the total return produced by an investment in the 500 U.S. stocks tracked by the Standard & Poor's 500 Index, with dividends reinvested.

Certainly it is true that spring always follows winter. It is equally true that buying stocks and holding on to them for long periods has a good chance of working out tolerably well because the general trend of stock prices since 1932 has been up. Each peak has been higher than the previous peak. But hanging around outside in winter, waiting for the spring, can be a chilling business. Doing it in the stock market can rob you of most of the profits you could have gained from better timing. It is, therefore, vital that you should be aware of the cycles of the market before venturing into it.

These cycles are not totally capricious, although at some point in your stock market travels you will undoubtedly think so. The rise and fall of stock prices in general have some connection to the ebb and flow of the economy. That is why long-term charts of the annual rate of growth in the economy show a similar pattern to charts of stock-price averages. The overall trend is up, but there are continual interruptions when the growth rate slows down and may even become a negative number representing a shrinking economy. These recurring fluctuations are known as business cycles. A period of expansion in the economy and a subsequent period of contraction make up a complete cycle. Note that only real growth is taken into account, that is, what's left after the effect of inflation on the actual numbers is removed.

Why industrial economies behave in this way and what to do to moderate the impact of the fluctuations on people's daily lives are highly controversial matters. The process by which one part of the cycle succeeds another is fairly well understood, but the timing and the original causes are not. A respectable collection of economic research suggests that over the long run the average business cycle lasts about four years, with an average advance of 30 months and an average decline of 19 months. But the average cycle since the Second World War appears to be lengthening to around five years. And those findings did not prevent the latest U.S. and Canadian expansions that began in 1983 from lasting an unusually long period of seven years, nor did they prevent the decline in Canada that began in November, 1979, from lasting a mere eight months.

Things are made more difficult by the fact that economic statistics are imperfect and are always being revised as new information comes in. It is fairly easy to identify the stages of the economic cycle through which we have already passed, but much harder to figure out what is going on right now. And the most difficult feat of all is to predict accurately what is going to happen next, as many a bruised economic forecaster can attest.

Fortunately, it is not necessary for a stock market investor to become an expert on all these economic controversies, although it can become an absorbing hobby. It is, however, useful to be aware of them in a general way and it is vital to have a good idea of where we have got to in the current cycle. Are we in the initial stages of expansion known as the recovery period, when the economy is still regaining the level of output it had reached before the previous decline? Are we in the full-flower period of expansion with economic output above the previous peak and rising? Is it late in the game, with the peak in economic output for this cycle approaching? Is it early in the slowdown, when output is still high and many people do not believe it is really happening? Or are we in the trough with output low, businessmen chastened or bankrupt, consumers depressed and unemployment high?

Even more important for investors, are we close to the end of one of these phases of the cycle? If so, stock prices are likely to begin anticipating the next phase, if they haven't already done so while we

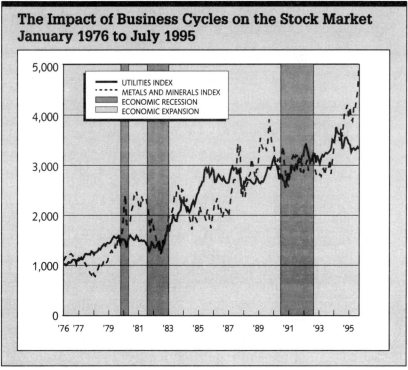

The Impact of Business Cycles on the Stock Market January 1976 to July 1995

UTILITIES INDEX
METALS AND MINERALS INDEX
ECONOMIC RECESSION
ECONOMIC EXPANSION

CHART VI

weren't looking. Late in the trough phase, prices start rising because investors expect the next phase to produce profit increases for companies and eventually higher dividends and bigger capital gains for the owners of their shares. Late in the expansion phase, stocks frequently turn down ahead of the economy for fear of the exact opposite. It is because of this behaviour that the stock market is seen as an advance indicator of the economy. Unfortunately, this is not as precise a process as it sounds. What happens from time to time is summed up in the often heard comment that the stock market has predicted 10 of the last five recessions. The market sends out many false signals as well as accurate ones. The trick is to identify which is which, something usually achieved by a combination of observation, experience and intuition, and sometimes only by luck.

Clearly, therefore, there are times to be in the stock market and times to stay out of it entirely; it's a matter of some importance not to get it the wrong way round. The meteoric rise and fall of Joseph Granville, probably the most colorful and self-promoting market-letter writer of the last decade, provides a cautionary tale. In the early 1980s, he became a superstar with the help of a well-timed call on the 1981-82 bear market and some antic behaviour that brought him massive publicity. At one public appearance in Arizona he appeared to walk on water, using a plank hidden below the surface of a swimming pool and told the audience afterward: "And now you know."

Other publicity stunts were even wilder, but they did seem to bring Granville influence over investors. On Jan. 6, 1981, a sell-everything message telephoned to a select group of his subscribers the previous midnight triggered a one-day price collapse on Wall Street, although prices recovered quickly and continued to march upward until around midyear. At that point they started falling again and a short-lived bear market really arrived. The trouble was that Granville's faithful subscribers were not let in on the good news when it came time to get back into stocks. The arrival, late in 1982, of the great bull market of the rest of the decade escaped his notice and for years afterward, to a diminishing audience, he continued to deny its existence.

In an eerie recent repetition, Robert Prechter, a much-publicized market analyst, acquired a reputation for genius by issuing a sell signal a few days before the record-breaking crash of October, 1987. But that reputation withered badly because of his failure to tell clients to get back in and ride the ensuing bull market upward.

How can you avoid such bad timing? Like the rest of us, you won't manage it all the time. But here are some suggestions.

Certainly a good time to stop buying stocks is in the late phases of an economic expansion as the peak approaches. By the time the peak has arrived, you should be selling off whatever stocks you have and hunkering down to wait out the bear market and the recession. Well into the trough period, though, the alert investor will begin to notice clues that indicate the recession is not really the end of civilization as we know it. Indeed, recovery is around the corner, although few believe in the prospect at that point. This is the time for you to begin picking up some of the bargains created by the earlier mass exodus of investors from the market.

Probably no one has described what you should do more felicitously than Fred Schwed Jr., in his 1940 stock market classic, *Where Are the Customers' Yachts?* "When there is a boom and everyone is scrambling for common stocks, take all your stocks and sell them," he wrote. "Put the proceeds in the bank. No doubt, the stocks you sold will go higher. Pay no attention to this — just wait for the recession which will come sooner or later. When it gets bad enough to arouse the politicians to make speeches, take your money out of the bank and buy back the stocks. No doubt the stocks will go still lower. Again pay no attention. Wait for the next boom. Continue to repeat this operation as long as you live, and you'll have the pleasure of dying rich."

This is, of course, a counsel of perfection, easier to describe than carry out. It is, in fact, very difficult to avoid buying stocks when everybody seems to be buying them, and equally hard to avoid selling them when everybody else seems to be doing that. Schwed's advice also ignores the possibility that the stocks you buy during the recession may be low in price for a good reason: The companies may be about to go bankrupt. That is why some investment advisers recommend against trying to time your entries and exits from the stock market according to cycles. They argue that you will usually get it wrong. Published studies have shown that missing a handful of the best days drastically reduces the rate of return received even in a long-running bull market. So you will be better off to use the buying-value strategy (see Chapter 11) or the diversification strategy (see Chapter 12). Remember, however, that if you always buy at market peaks and sell at market troughs, you will have to be an extraordinarily good picker of individual stocks to make much money.

Another reason for being aware of where we are in the business cycle is the fact that different types of stocks do well in different phases. As the economy waxes and wanes, a succession of stock groups find a place in the sun for a while, then fall from grace. For instance, when the economy slows down and interest rates start to decline, so-called defensive stocks usually come into favour. These include stocks that are bought mainly for their large and dependable dividend payments such as shares of the major Canadian banks and natural gas and telephone utilities. This group also includes retail grocery chains and suppliers of basic foods on the argument that while consumers may stop spending on frivolous items such as fashion goods and foreign holidays, they will not cut back dramatically on essentials such as groceries.

The rise and fall of the Canadian stock market is strongly influenced by the individual cycle of such natural-resource stocks as the mining companies. They are always hit very badly in an economic recession and are slow starters in an ensuing economic recovery. But they come on very strongly in the latter stages of an expansion, providing a late-season party for those bold enough to climb aboard early. Because Canadian analysts and investors are usually more closely attuned to the mining industry's fortunes, there is a recurring scenario in which they happily buy the mining stocks at fairly low prices and later sell them to excited U.S. investors at high prices. Oil and gas stocks used to show a similar pattern, but these days their prices vary with the success or failure of the efforts of the Organization of Petroleum Exporting Countries' cartel at maintaining the international price of crude oil, and the worldwide balance of supply and demand for oil. If you own such stocks, or are thinking of buying some, you must brief yourself on these matters.

If you assume that you can identify where we are in the current business cycle with reasonable accuracy, how can you go about capitalizing on this assessment? Your first decision, of course, is whether to own any stocks at all. For most of the cycle you probably should, but in varying proportions of your total savings. Late in a recession you should begin loading up on solid blue-chip stocks of companies that have come through the downturn in reasonably good shape. They will be the first to recover as investors regain confidence that better economic times will soon return. You can then stay fairly fully invested in stocks until the late phase of the cycle, up to your chosen limit, which should vary according to your age, investment objectives and tolerance of risk. Telltale signs that it's getting late in the day include magazine cover stories on big stock market winners, business page features explaining why this bull market will go on forever because it is different from all its predecessors and constant gossip in restaurants and elevators about the latest hot stock. At that time, you should be quietly taking your well-deserved profits and reducing the size of your stock portfolio.

To take maximum advantage of the cyclical changes in the investment environment, you should switch from stock group to stock group, preferably just ahead of when investors' interest switches from one group to another. One way of going about this is through overweighting and underweighting your portfolio in relation to, say, the TSE's composite index of 300 representative stocks. The exchange publishes statistics that show the relative weighting of individual stock groups in the index.

Toronto Stock Exchange Subindex Weights
AS A PERCENTAGE OF THE TSE 300

Metals and minerals	9.26	**Real estate**	0.27
Integrated mines	6.51		
Mining	2.74	**Transportation and environmental**	
		services	1.53
Gold and precious minerals	11.00		
		Pipelines	2.33
Oil and gas	12.26		
Integrated oils	3.02	**Utilities**	9.03
Oil and gas producers	9.13	Telephone utilities	7.25
Oil and gas services	0.11	Gas/electric utilities	1.78
Paper and forest	4.16	**Communications and media**	3.27
		Broadcasting	0.37
Consumer products	6.84	Cable and entertainment	0.82
Food processing	0.13	Publishing and printing	2.08
Tobacco	1.12		
Distilleries	3.15	**Merchandising**	3.53
Breweries and beverages	0.53	Wholesale distributors	0.42
Household goods	0.51	Food stores	1.03
Biotechnology/		Department stores	0.35
pharmaceuticals	1.40	Specialty stores	0.59
		Hospitality	1.14
Industrial products	16.96		
Steel	1.13	**Financial services**	15.41
Fabricating and engineering	0.95	Banks and trusts	12.80
Transportation equipment	1.58	Investment cos. and funds	1.06
Technology - hardware	5.92	Insurance	0.71
Building materials	0.54	Financial management	0.84
Chemicals and fertilizers	4.39		
Technology - software	0.94		
Autos and parts	1.51	**Conglomerates**	4.14

JUNE 28, 1996   SOURCE: TORONTO STOCK EXCHANGE

TABLE VII

The huge portfolios handled by professional money managers are frequently invested in all of these groups and their strategy is to raise and lower the proportions of particular groups by a few percentage points, in accordance with their view of the current investment environment. It is unlikely that you will ever have a personal portfolio large enough to require handling in that way, but you can follow the principle in a rough and ready fashion, if you wish.

Suppose, for instance, that you believe the sun is about to shine once more on mining and oil stocks, but that it is setting for financial services and telephone utilities stocks. You could perhaps triple the TSE index weightings for the coming favourites and halve the weightings for the new Cinderellas. Based on weightings in mid-1996, you would end up with approximately 28 per cent of your portfolio in the mines and another 37 per cent in the oils. Another 12 per cent would be in financial services and utilities, and the remaining 23 per cent could be split among other groups, such as industrial and consumer products.

Again, this is harder than it sounds. Dancing your way aggressively and unscathed through business and market cycles is just about the hardest thing to try in the stock market. Many have tried but few have succeeded. John Maynard Keynes, the brilliant English economist and successful stock market speculator who threw new light on how the business cycle actually works, wrote that in 20 years of observation, he had not seen a single successful instance of it. Maybe you are an exception and can take maximum advantage of the fickle fancies of the crowd to make big money consistently. The odds are against you, though. The best that most of us can do is to be sufficiently aware of the rhythm to know when stocks are what you should own and when you should avoid them like the plague.

CHAPTER 8

Fundamental Thinking

ASKED WHY SHE BOUGHT ABC Enterprises and not XYZ Enterprises, an investor may reply that ABC is exploiting more effectively the opportunities offered by a changing industry, that its profit is growing more quickly and that it is in better financial shape. Asked why she considered buying stocks in that industry in the first place, the investor may say it's an industry that will benefit from the expanding economy and lower interest rates she expects over the next 12 months. Those answers indicate this investor is using the fundamental approach to picking stocks. She is looking at the facts and figures behind a company's performance, and the environment in which it operates, to decide whether its stock is a good bet. This is a time-honoured and serious-minded technique. The first edition of the classic textbook on the subject, Benjamin Graham's *Security Analysis*, was published in 1934. A more recent edition, published in 1962, ran to 778 pages of closely reasoned prose, tables and charts. Often enough, it even works.

Fundamental analysis can be as simple and basic as finding out what type of business the company is in and whether it's making money at it. Amazingly, some stock buyers don't even go that far. The technique can also be as intellectually demanding as figuring out how much of a company's profit comes from business success and how much from adroitly timed accounting changes. How can that be so, you may ask? A profit is a profit, isn't it? Alas, no. A profit is actually part fact and part opinion. Let's look more closely.

The most detailed financial information about a company available to investors in the normal course of events is contained in its annual report. More detailed information is filed for many companies with the U.S. Securities & Exchange Commission in Washington, but that probably won't come your way often. You are entitled to receive an annual report in the mail if you own some of a firm's publicly traded shares. Even if you are not a shareholder, most big companies will send you one if you ask, in the hope you will become a shareholder or at least buy one of their products or services. In the section of the report devoted to the financial statements you will find the income statement, to which you have already been introduced in Chapter 4. This is the one that tells you whether the company is running a profitable business, a rather important fact.

Take a look at the sample income statement of Anderson Enterprises Inc., a fictional company, on the opposite page. Some of the items listed are easy to follow. Look at total sales on the second line. Good, they went up last year. And there are the operating expenses. Oh, oh. Not so good. They're up, too, and by more than sales, it seems. As a result, the operating profit (line 6), which is what's left after subtracting the operating expenses from the sales, is down from the previous year. But look at this; interest expenses (line 10) are down from last year. That's better. A bit farther down there's the income-tax bill (lines 12 and 13), which seems clear enough on the face of it but reveals some complications upon closer scrutiny. The total tax bill is divided into two portions, current and deferred. That needs investigating. And what's this big expense called depreciation (line 8)? And this smaller one called amortization of goodwill (line 9)? And how can the company lose money and make money at the same time, before extraordinary items (line 15) and after extraordinary items (line 18)? What are extraordinary items on line 17, anyway? And can we learn much about how Anderson Enterprises is doing from this statement?

Indeed we can, but the first and most important thing you should note is that the figures in isolation don't tell you much. In fact, they can be quite misleading. The relationships between the figures are what you have to check. If you look only at the increased sales figures of Anderson Enterprises and at the line showing net profit after extraordinary items, you might think the company is doing not too badly. Sales are up 34 per cent and it's profitable. When you take operating expenses into account, however, it's clear the management has some big problems. The major expenses of running the company are rising much faster than sales. To keep track of this key relationship, you calculate how much of each dollar in sales goes to pay those expenses. The answer is expressed as a percentage and is usually called the operating profit margin (line 7). In the case of Anderson Enterprises, this figure was 11 per cent in its latest fiscal

Anderson Enterprises Inc.
Statement of Income

1. Year ended June 30	1996	1995	% Change
2. Sales	$36,477,480	$27,222,000	34
3. Cost of goods sold	25,534,236	17,694,300	44
4. (Gross profit margin)	30%	35%	
5. Selling, admin. & general	6,823,000	3,266,237	109
6. Operating profit	4,120,244	6,261,463	−34
7. (Operating profit margin)	11%	23%	
8. Depreciation	2,900,000	2,265,000	28
9. Amortization of goodwill	862,000	978,600	−12
10. Interest	842,985	936,650	−10
11. Net profit before tax	-484,741	2,081,213	
12. Current income taxes	-10,666	392,728	
13. Deferred income taxes	-15,233	856,000	
14. (Tax rate)		40%	
15. Net earnings after tax (before extraordinary items)	-458,842	832,485	
16. (Net profit margin)	N.A.	3%	
17. Extraordinary items	1,200,000	-	
18. Net earnings after tax (after extraordinary items)	741,158	832,485	−11
19. Preferred dividends	40,000	40,000	

TABLE VIII

year and 23 per cent the previous year. That means the company spent 89 cents of every sales dollar on operating expenses last year, up from 77 cents, which is not a good sign.

It may be, of course, that 1995 was a year in which special circumstances threw expenses off track. To get some perspective on this, you should always look back further than just the most recent two years. Five years is generally accepted as a reasonable history for assessing a company's recent performance. A check of a five-year summary of key ratios of Anderson Enterprises might show you that until 1995 the company had been steadily improving its operating profit margin. What went wrong and will there be similar problems this year? You have to follow up on the clues provided by a company's financial statements to answer such vital questions. For instance, many companies break down operating expenses into the cost of goods sold and the selling, administrative and general expenses, and it may be that the problem was concentrated in one or other of these categories. This would be discovered by calculating the ratio between each category and total sales.

Unfortunately, the management of Anderson Enterprises appears to have problems in both categories. Its cost of goods sold (line 3) increased 44 per cent last year while sales rose only 34 per cent. As a result, what the company had left out of each dollar of sales after covering the cost of goods sold fell to 30 cents from 35 cents the previous year. Comparisons of this figure, called the gross profit margin and usually given as a percentage (line 4), with results achieved by other companies in the same industry are a good way to judge the effectiveness of management at its basic business. To see how good management is at controlling general costs you should bring the selling, administrative and general expenses into the picture by calculating the operating profit margin. Again, the management of Anderson Enterprises needs to keep a tighter grip. Those expenses jumped a dangerously large 109 per cent last year, a development that was a big factor in dragging down its operating profit margin. Worse, the overall impact of lax cost control more than offset the company's lower interest bills and helped slash to zero from 3 per cent the most important income-statement ratio of all, the net profit margin after taxes (line 16). This last ratio is the figure that most effectively sums up the management's ability to run its business.

The reasons behind these problems may be difficult to discover and it is more the business of professional investment analysts to find them. The point is that by checking on the operating profit margin of Anderson Enterprises, you would be alerted to the need to ask some questions about its management's competence before investing in its shares. You can calculate these and other key measures of performance yourself from a company's annual reports and from its interim statements, usually published every three months (see Calculation Formulas for Key Ratios). Some companies provide the ratios themselves in their published reports, although they are not obliged to do so. They are also available from sources specializing in providing information for investors and analysts, including computer on-line services.

Sales revenue and operating expenses are, of course, facts and not opinion, although even sales can evaporate if a customer does not pay for goods ordered. There are items on a company's financial statements, however, that do not exist in any other form except as entries in the books. These items were created by accountants not to mystify but to inform. They are there to avoid presenting a misleading picture of how a company is doing.

Take depreciation, for instance. Physical assets owned by a company — machinery, equipment, buildings, furniture, vehicles — lose their value with time and use, and that loss is just as much a cost of doing business as employees' wages. If it wasn't reflected on the financial statements, a company's profit would be overstated. An amount is therefore deducted from a company's revenue to reflect it, before the profit is calculated. Because this is not an actual amount spent, various formulas are used to calculate the deduction, all based on the estimated useful life of the class of asset being depreciated. A building is considered to have a longer useful life than a company-owned car, for instance. And because depreciation charges reduce the amount of profit subject to corporate income tax, the tax authorities lay down rules limiting the maximum amount that can be deducted for tax purposes. The cumulative amount of depreciation is shown on the company's balance sheet as a deduction from the value of fixed assets it owns. It's important to realize, however, that no money is actually set aside by the company as a sort of replacement fund. If it were, the cumulative amount would be shown as an asset on the balance sheet, not as a reduction in asset value. Depreciation is purely a bookkeeping figure designed to allocate the cost of an asset used in the business over its useful life.

As well as a depreciation charge, the income statement of Anderson Enterprises has an item called amortization of goodwill. This, too, is deducted as an expense before profit is calculated, but it also is strictly a bookkeeping amount. Goodwill is classified as an intangible asset because, unlike cash, inventories or buildings, you can't see and touch it. It appears most frequently as a result of an acquisition of another business for a price that is greater than the value shown on the books of that business. The practice is to take the assets and liabilities of the acquired business on to the purchasing company's books at their stated values, and to show the difference as goodwill. If nothing else were done, though, the cost of acquiring that intangible asset would not be reflected at all. Today's accounting rules provide, however, for the cost to be reflected or amortized over a period of time. Again, no money is actually set aside. The charge is just a bookkeeping figure that is subject to wide discretion.

Calculation Formulas for Key Ratios

$$\text{Gross profit margin} = \frac{\text{Net sales less cost of goods sold}}{\text{Net sales}} \times 100$$

$$\text{Operating profit margin} = \frac{\text{Net sales} - (\text{cost of goods sold and other expenses})}{\text{Net sales}} \times 100$$

$$\text{Net profit margin (after tax)} = \frac{\text{Net earnings (before extraordinary items)} + \text{minority interests}}{\text{Net sales}} \times 100$$

$$\text{Working capital ratio} = \frac{\text{Current assets}}{\text{Current liabilities}}$$

$$\text{Debt/equity ratio} = \frac{\text{Total debt outstanding (including short- and long-term)}}{\text{Book value of shareholders' equity}} \times 100$$

$$\text{Net after-tax return on invested capital} = \frac{\text{Net earnings (before extraordinary items)} + \text{interest (after tax)}}{\text{Invested capital (debt plus equity)}} \times 100$$

$$\text{Net after-tax return on equity} = \frac{\text{Net earnings (before extraordinary items)} - \text{preferred dividends}}{\text{Common equity}} \times 100$$

$$\text{Ratio of cash flow from operations to total debt} = \frac{\text{Cash flow from operations (including non-cash deductions from profit)}}{\text{Total debt outstanding (short- and long-term)}} \times 100$$

$$\text{Book value or equity per common share} = \frac{\text{Shareholders' equity} - \text{preferred share capital}}{\text{Number of common shares outstanding}}$$

$$\text{Earnings per common share} = \frac{\text{Net earnings (before extraordinary items)} - \text{preferred dividends}}{\text{Number of common shares outstanding}}$$

$$\text{Price-earnings ratio or P/E multiple} = \frac{\text{Current market price of common share}}{\text{Earnings per share (latest 12-month period)}}$$

$$\text{Dividend yield} = \frac{\text{Indicated annual dividend per share (\$)}}{\text{Current market price}} \times 100$$

TABLE IX

Assessing the treatment of depreciation and amortization charges by various companies is also mostly a matter for expert investment analysts. You will usually not be equipped to judge whether the amount provided for depreciation is excessively large or imprudently small. Nor will you usually be able to judge whether the profit is being overstated or understated because of provisions for amortization of goodwill or some of the more exotic entries you will find on some companies' financial statements. What's important is that you should be sufficiently aware of such possibilities to be able to ask questions if you encounter something you don't understand.

The financial statements of companies with shares traded on the stock market must be accompanied by a certificate of authenticity from an independent firm of chartered accountants, which you can read for yourself in a company's annual report. But all this auditors' certificate guarantees is that the statements were prepared "in accordance with generally accepted accounting principles applied on a basis consistent with that of the preceding year." The principles this wording refers to are laid down by the accountants' professional organization, the Canadian Institute of Chartered Accountants, and represent an honest attempt to help its members present a company's financial position fairly. But inevitably these rules allow for a wide range of discretion in reporting certain items, and honest people can differ over them in ways that have a big impact on the bottom line. Equally inevitably, there are less scrupulous corporate executives who keep congenial company with the sort of accountant who, when asked what the net profit is, replies: "What number would you like?" Life is too short to keep up with their machinations, so steer well clear of the shares of companies where you come across such unholy alliances. The specialist financial publications are a good source of information about the most blatant examples.

Moving farther down the earnings statement of Anderson Enterprises, you will come to provisions for income tax. These are of two kinds, current and deferred. The company appeared in 1995 to be in the happy position of being able to put off paying some of its tax bills. Why? Because tax as reported on a company's tax return and paid to the government can be, and frequently is, different from the amount of tax calculated on its financial statements in accordance with accounting guidelines. Usually, the tax paid is a smaller amount, and what isn't actually paid is reported as deferred tax. Depending on the reason for the deferment, some or all of this may never be paid. In any case, the cumulative amount of deferred taxes

Anderson Enterprises Inc.
Balance Sheet for 1996
At June 30, 1996

ASSETS

20.	Current assets		
21.	Cash and bank balances		$ 165,000
22.	Marketable securities		1,005,000
23.	Accounts receivable		927,000
24.	Inventories		2,655,000
25.	Prepaid expenses		128,000
26.	Total current assets		4,880,000
27.	Investment in affiliate		2,000,000
28.	Fixed assets		
29.	Buildings	5,665,000	
30.	Equipment	12,650,000	
31.		18,315,000	
32.	Accumulated depreciation	6,318,000	11,997,000
33.	Land		1,250,000
34.	Deferred charges		165,000
35.	Goodwill		2,170,000
36.	Total assets		22,462,000

LIABILITIES

37.	Current liabilities	
38.	Bank loans	1,630,000
39.	Accounts payable	1,271,950
40.	Income taxes payable	45,000
41.	Bonds due	200,000
42.	Total current liabilities	3,146,950
43.	Deferred income taxes	585,000
44.	Long-term debt	5,575,000

SHAREHOLDERS' EQUITY

45.	Preferred shares	500,000
46.	Common shares	2,000,000
47.	Retained earnings	10,655,050
48.	Total equity	13,155,050
49.	Total liabilities	22,462,000
50.	Working capital ratio	1.55
51.	Debt/equity ratio	56%
52.	Net return on invested capital	NA
53.	Net return on equity	NA

TABLE X

Anderson Enterprises Inc.
Statement of Changes in Financial Position

	Fiscal 1996
54. Net earnings after tax	$ -458,842
(before extraordinary items)	
55. Depreciation	2,900,000
56. Amortization of goodwill	862,000
57. Deferred income taxes	(15,233)
58. Cash flow from operations	3,287,925
59. Increase (decrease) in long-term debt	(120,000)
60. Sale of fixed assets	1,985,000
61. Total cash flow	5,152,925
Dividends paid	
62. Preferred	40,000
63. Common	200,000
64. Capital investments	1,875,000
	2,115,000
65. Net cash provided	3,037,925

TABLE XI

over the years is shown on the company's balance sheet as a separate liability.

After showing both current and deferred income taxes, Anderson Enterprises shows its net earnings after tax but before extraordinary items (line 15), if any. Although this is not physically the last line of the earnings statement, it is the fabled bottom line by which corporate management stands or falls. This is what is left from operating the business to reward shareholders, after all expenses have been paid or provided for. Some or all will almost certainly be retained by the business to provide capital for expanded operations. Some or all of it may be paid out to shareholders as dividends. If 1996's disappointing results continue, the shareholders of Anderson Enterprises will soon face a cut in dividends. It paid $40,000 to preferred shareholders (lines 19 and 63) and $200,000 to its common shareholders (line 63) in 1995.

According to the figures on line 18 of the company's financial statements, Anderson Enterprises remained profitable in 1996, despite all its problems. This occurred because of a large income item that represented the net capital gain made by the company on the expropriation by a municipality of some land owned by the company. Such profits are not part of the normal business activities of the company and are beyond the control of its management. So including them in its regular income would distort the results for the year. They are therefore separated and investment analysts ignore them when assessing a company's profit performance. Extraordinary or non-recurring items are all of this nature.

To round out the picture of how Anderson Enterprises is doing requires a look at the company's balance sheet, shown on page 70. Unlike the income statement, which is a report of what happened over a period of time, a balance sheet is a snapshot of a company's financial condition at one particular time, usually the last day of an accounting period. This means that a balance sheet for the day before, or the day after, could be quite different. The company's income statement and its cash flow statement of changes in financial position tell the continuing story of what happened between balance-sheet dates.

Balance sheets are easier to follow than you might think, once you understand their simple basic arithmetic. The procedure consists of first summarizing a company's assets, that is, what it owns and what is owed to it. Then liabilities, or what the company owes, are summarized. Liabilities are then subtracted from assets and what's left is called the equity and is considered to belong to the shareholders. Thus, the balance sheet of Anderson Enterprises shows total assets of $22.5 million (line 36) and total liabilities before shareholders' equity of $9.3 million. That leaves $13.2 million that belongs to the shareholders (line 48). Some assets and liabilities are classified as current. On the asset side, these include cash (line 21) and items such as marketable securities (line 22) that can be turned into cash quickly, plus items such as accounts receivable (line 23) and inventories (line 24) expected to become cash in the normal course of business before the end of the next accounting year. Current liabilities (line 37) are items due for payment during the next accounting year, such as short-term bank loans (line 38) and accounts payable (line 39).

Investment analysts use combinations of figures from the income statement and the balance sheet to help them assess how a company is faring. The calculation you will encounter most frequently is that which shows how much profit a company's management is able to earn on each dollar of equity invested in the business by the owners of its common shares. In the case of Anderson Enterprises, the answer is zero. A profit is usually expressed as a percentage and called the return on equity. This figure is calculated by adding together the stated capital of common shares ($2 million for Anderson Enterprises) and the retained earnings ($10.7 million), then figuring out what the net after-tax profit available for common shareholders represents as a percentage of that total. Any preferred-share dividend payments are deducted from the net profit after tax.

A drawback of using this figure to compare one company's performance with another is that each company may have different proportions of common equity, equity belonging to preferred shareholders and borrowed long-term capital. Therefore, some analysts prefer a more complicated calculation of how much a company earns on its total invested capital — the amount provided by loans and by common and preferred shareholders. This involves adding back to the net profit after tax an amount that represents the effective after-tax cost of interest payments. That total is then calculated as a percentage of the invested capital.

A balance sheet can also flash warnings of impending financial trouble. For instance, any business needs working capital to pay wages, suppliers and other bills before money comes in from customers. The working capital ratio tracks whether the company is running into danger. It is calculated by dividing the current assets by the current liabilities. Anderson Enterprises has a ratio of 1.55, which means it has $1.55 in cash and other current assets to pay each dollar of short-term debts. This is not a desperate situation, but if this ratio keeps falling, it could become so. Such a problem would be made worse if the company's debt-to-equity ratio rises from its current 56 per cent. This figure tells us that Anderson Enterprises owes 56 cents for each dollar of shareholders' equity, including preferred shares. It's a measure of financial risk. The higher the figure, the higher the risk.

A company's financial fortunes are also reflected in its statement of changes in financial position, sometimes known as the cash flow statement. This statement tracks all the cash flowing into and out of the company, for whatever reason. As we have seen, there can be large deductions on the income statement that are not actual cash expenses, such as depreciation, amortization or deferred taxes. The cash-flow statement adds back those items to arrive at a total of cash provided from the company's business operations. It also includes cash that comes in from additional borrowing and from the sale of additional shares. Similarly, cash can be spent on items that are not recorded as expenses on the income statement. These include re-payments of loans, the purchase of new capital equipment or other investments, payments of dividends and a long list of other reasons for which a company may issue a cheque.

Close study of cash flow statements can reveal the answer to such mysteries as how a company that, according to its income state-ment, has little or no profit can still pay its bills and even thrive: It has large depreciation charges or other bookkeeping write-offs. These statements can also warn you that a company is staying afloat only by running up more and more loans from a tolerant or foolish banker. In such a case, the ratio of cash flow to total debts will be falling. This calculation expresses a company's cash flow from op-erations as a percentage of the total amount of its debts in all forms. Anderson Enterprises has a figure of 44 per cent. Investors in this company should keep a watchful eye out for declines in this per-centage. It is comfortably above the generally accepted minimum for industrial companies of 30 per cent, but you never know.

Is this sort of analysis worth the effort? Yes, as long as you re-member that you are gathering clues to the future, not guarantees. No one can be certain that a company that has done well for the past five years will do equally well next year. Business history is full of winners that eventually turned into losers, and conversely many an ugly duckling has become a swan. All that can be said is that the odds are better with the five-year winner than with the five-year loser.

A great deal also depends on the prospects for the industry in which a company is involved. There can be well-managed compa-nies in industries that are declining, and there can be poorly man-aged companies in industries with bright prospects. The techniques of fundamental analysis enable you to recognize which is which. You compare the performance ratios of the company you are ana-lyzing with its previous performance to see whether it is doing bet-ter, worse or about the same. And you compare its performance ratios with industry averages to see whether it's ahead of the pack or behind. With that knowledge, you are better equipped than most stock market players to make an intelligent investment decision.

CHAPTER 9

The Technical Approach

WHEN THE TORONTO STOCK
Exchange opened for business on Monday, Oct. 19, 1987, the price
for one share of Alcan Aluminium Ltd. was $42.75. One week later,
the opening price for one Alcan share was $29. On the face of it, in
just seven days something had happened to slice more than $2 bil-
lion off the market value of one of Canada's leading industrial companies. But what? A check of the record shows no untoward change
in the business fortunes of Alcan during those seven days. No strike
shut down its operations. No government nationalized its operations without compensation. Nobody won a multimillion-dollar liability suit against it. The company continued serenely on its way
to making a large profit of $433 million (U.S.) for the year.

At the start of that highly successful year, Alcan shares were trading at around $39, which implied the company was worth just over
$6 billion. At the highest price at which the shares traded during
1987, $49.50 in early October, the stock market valued the company
at close to $8 billion. At the lowest price of $26 in late October, the
stock market valued the company at not much more than half that
figure. The year-end valuation: $6 billion again, based on a stock
price of $37. Was there any justification based on fundamental
analysis of the company's business operations for these wide swings
in the market's valuation? Hardly. Throughout the year, the company reported successively higher profits of 39 cents a share in the
first quarter, 60 cents in the second quarter, 72 cents in the third
quarter and 81 cents in the final three months.

This sort of fickle assessment was not confined to Alcan. As 1987
began, the TSE 300 composite index was just a fraction above 3000.
At its high point during the year it had surpassed 4000, but at its
low it had fallen back to around 2800, well below its starting point.
As the year ended, it had climbed back to about 3200. Those swings

represented changes of many billions of dollars in investors' valuations of the companies in the index.

Such big variations in the market's valuations of companies are the Achilles' heel of fundamental analysts. Clearly, something else is going on in the stock market, something more than a cool, rational assessment of what companies are worth, based on the statistics of their business performance. Enter the technical analyst, who argues that trying to put an intrinsic value on a stock certificate is a fool's game. What needs to be studied, so the argument goes, is the action of the market itself. For the dedicated technical analyst, no value but today's market price exists. A stock is worth no more and no less than that price. Of course, it may be worth more tomorrow and less next week, but that will be decided by investor supply and demand, reflected in daily market transactions and crystallized in the form of the current auction price that emerges on stock exchanges.

Technical analysts agree that valuations based on fundamental analysis play a role in the daily market drama, but not the starring role. The drama is played out by a cast of multitudes, acting in hope or fear according to their needs and resources, behaving rationally one moment and irrationally the next. By definition, it is impossible to analyze this complex swirl of factors. No statistics are available to keep track of them except the price at which transactions occur and the number of transactions. It is on these statistics that the science of technical analysis is founded. The history of trading in a particular stock or in market averages is recorded, usually on a chart, and from the picture created by that chart the technical analyst reaches conclusions about what is likely to happen next.

Technical analysts also argue that most of the statistics studied by fundamental analysts are irrelevant to the key question of what is likely to happen next. In a classic textbook on the subject, *Technical Analysis of Stock Trends*, by Robert Edwards and John Magee, the point is made this way: "[The market] is constantly looking ahead; attempting to discount future developments, weighing and balancing all the estimates and guesses of hundreds of investors who look into the future from different points of view and through glasses of many different hues." That being so, the authors say, "the going price as established by the market itself comprehends all the fundamental information which the statistical analyst can hope to learn (plus some which is perhaps secret from him, known only to a few insiders) and much else besides of equal or even greater impor-tance."

These arguments, even if accepted, are not enough to make the case for using technical analysis to play the market. The technique would be a waste of effort unless it were possible to show that there is some real-world relationship between the future and previous market movements as portrayed in the charts. It is not enough for a fortuneteller to point out the patterns left by tea leaves in a drained cup. The customer must be persuaded that those patterns provide accurate predictions. Similarly, all the intriguing chart patterns in the world are of little value to the investor if they cannot be used to help make a decision about whether to buy or sell.

Fortunately, there is evidence that they can, at least to a limited extent. You don't have to look at many stock-price charts to realize that, although prices vary from day to day, they tend to move in clearly discernible trends over longer periods of time. Stocks hardly ever go straight up or straight down. Like the tides, they advance or retreat in a series of waves until advance gives way to retreat at the high-water mark, or vice versa. They may also, unlike the tides, stay in more or less the same place for a while, their prices still showing a wavelike pattern on the chart, then suddenly break out of this re-petitive pattern by moving upward or downward.

Strikingly, this is as true of today's stocks as of those of the 1960s or the 1930s. Only the names and the trading volumes have changed. What is at work here is human nature and the psychology of crowds, which seems never to change. Clearly, there is money to be made by market players who recognize a high-water mark, a low-water mark or a breakout before the rest of the crowd. Technical analysts offer this prospect to investors. They spend their time and talents studying patterns on their charts that produce signals of when to buy or sell. The good ones do not claim that their signals are infallible. They merely say that acting on predictions based on the patterns of previous trading offers better odds of success than other methods. As always, you should distrust market seers who claim infallibility. Pride usually goes before a fall, especially in the stock market.

The most used working tools of technical analysts are charts. These come in a multitude of forms, but the most common is a bar chart showing previous market prices and trading volume. The hori-zontal axis represents a period of time. The upper portion of the

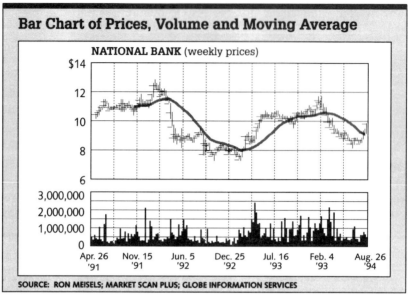

Bar Chart of Prices, Volume and Moving Average

NATIONAL BANK (weekly prices)

SOURCE: RON MEISELS; MARKET SCAN PLUS; GLOBE INFORMATION SERVICES

CHART VII

vertical axis represents the price, and the lower portion the number of shares traded. Prices may be plotted daily, weekly, monthly or yearly. Typically, a vertical bar is used to represent the highest and lowest prices during a period. A horizontal tick on the bar records the price of the last transaction in the period, also known as the closing price. This price is important because it represents the market's final evaluation of the stock in the period charted, and it is the figure noted and remembered by most investors. The volume of trading is recorded as a vertical bar rising from the base line of the chart.

The vertical price axis may be a simple arithmetic scale, with equal amounts of space for equal amounts of dollars. The distance between $20 and $30 is the same as between $10 and $20. This provides a misleading picture of percentage changes in the price, however. A stock that moves from $10 to $20 has made a 100 per cent gain, but a stock that moves from $20 to $30 has risen only 50 per cent. A more accurate picture of price changes is provided by a semi-logarithmic scale, which allocates the same amount of space for a move from $20 to $40 as for a move from $10 to $20. It is the percentage gain on your money that counts, after all. The volume of trading is, however, plotted on an arithmetic scale.

Point and Figure Chart

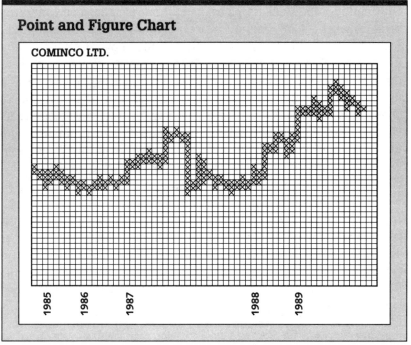

COMINCO LTD.

1985 1986 1987 1988 1989

CHART VIII

One problem with the bar chart is that much energy and time can be wasted plotting the price of a stock that hardly moves. Little useful information is gained from such a picture. A different sort of chart, called point-and-figure, eliminates this problem. Like the bar chart, this one has a vertical axis to show the price. The horizontal axis also shows the time elapsed, but not to scale. Graph paper is always used and nothing is plotted on this chart until the price moves to fixed points, like an elevator opening its doors only when a particular floor is reached, not between floors.

Suppose you are charting a stock that is trading at $24.75 and you choose to use an interval of one point or $1. You do not enter anything on the chart until the stock moves either to $25 or to $24. Usually, all transaction prices are checked in point-and-figure charting, not just the high, low and closing prices. Each time the stock trades at a round-dollar price an X is plotted on the chart. All other prices are ignored. Suppose the stock moves up to $26. You will already have entered an X when it first traded at $25. Now you enter a second X directly above the first one. If the stock then moves to $27, you enter a third X in the same column directly above the second X.

Now suppose the stock drops back and trades at $26. You can't drop back down the same column to record this because the square directly below is already occupied. So you move over to the next column to record the change in direction. This process continues as the stock trades at different prices, with the chartist entering X's in new columns only when the direction of the price movement changes (see Chart VIII). The $1 interval is the most commonly used. In Canada, where markets are frequently slower moving, and for stocks trading below $20, some chartists use 50-cent price intervals. Point-and-figure chartists ignore trading-volume figures because they believe a one-point price change would not occur without significant trading volume.

The technique means that a point-and-figure chart will ignore periods in which there is not much going on, but faithfully capture the action when things get more lively. This means a single chart can cover long periods of time and still convey all the essential information. As a result, many professional technical analysts prefer them. However, the difficulty in understanding the technique makes them less popular among investors. It can also be difficult for non-professionals to obtain the information needed to check all prices at which a stock trades during a session. There are services available in the U.S. that supply finished point-and-figure charts, but none in Canada yet. As a result, some chartists compromise and use closing prices.

You can plot your own standard bar charts from the stock quotations published in newspapers. You can create and print them, using a computer and modem to obtain prices and trading volumes from an on-line information service. Computer software is available to speed up and virtually automate this chore. You can also buy ready-made charts for the stocks in which you are interested, with regular updates available to order. Charts of various market indexes and averages are also available from the same sources. A Canadian investor will usually want to follow the movements of the TSE 300 index and at least some of its component subindexes.

Indexes are the most common form of statistical measures of market performance. They are calculated in various ways but they all reflect percentage gains or losses in relation to a base period. Curiously, though, the world's best-known market indicator, the Dow Jones industrial, is an adjusted average, not an index. It does not give a representative picture of price changes on the New York

Head-and-Shoulder Daily Chart

CANADIAN TIRE 'A'

NECKLINE

SOURCE: RON MEISELS; MARKET SCAN PLUS; GLOBE INFORMATION SERVICES

CHART IX

Stock Exchange and the way it is calculated attracts a lot of criticism. Despite the Dow's shortcomings, however, it is necessary for investors to pay some attention to its movements. Why? Principally because everybody else is doing so. Even investors who play the game by being contrary and taking the opposite view to the crowd need to know what the crowd is up to. This applies especially to those who seek to use technical analysis to help make buying or selling decisions. Signals flashed by the movements of the average and of its close cousins, the transportation, utility and composite averages also published by the New York-based Dow Jones & Co., are monitored and frequently acted on by a host of market players.

What sort of signals? Frequently, they are the same as those a technical analyst looks for in individual stock-price charts: patterns that suggest one trend is over and another is beginning. The most famous of these so-called reversal patterns is the head-and-shoulders (see Chart IX). Depending on whether they are right-side-up or inverted, these can signal either that a stock that has been going up for a while has now started to fall, or that a previously falling stock has begun an upward climb. If reliable, this is important information for any investor to have.

The right-side-up pattern begins with a minor fall-back on slower trading volume in a stock that has been rising strongly for a while,

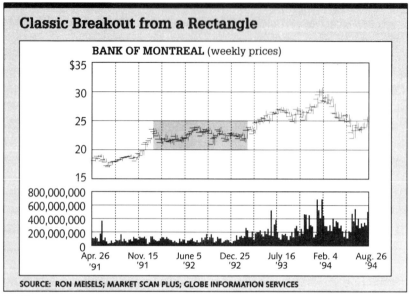

Classic Breakout from a Rectangle

BANK OF MONTREAL (weekly prices)

SOURCE: RON MEISELS; MARKET SCAN PLUS; GLOBE INFORMATION SERVICES

CHART X

followed by an upward move that carries the price beyond the previous peak. There is nothing unusual in that, of course. The stock has probably been moving in a similar pattern all the way up. But what happens next offers the first clue that this time it's going to be different. The stock falls back, usually on slower trading volume, to somewhere around the bottom of the first fall-back — that is, below the top of what now appears to be the probable left shoulder. Then a third rally occurs that fails to reach the height of the second rally, or head, and which is accompanied by much lower trading volume. This upward move forms the right shoulder. In the subsequent decline the price falls below the so-called neckline, a line drawn on the chart connecting the lowest prices reached during the two fall-backs, which confirms to technical analysts that the price trend has changed from up to down. Often, there is further confirmation when the price bounces back up to the neckline, only to start its downward trek again. An inverted head-and-shoulders pattern happens the opposite way round and signals that the price trend has changed from down to up.

The rectangle is another frequently seen chart pattern. It occurs when a stock price moves up and down between clearly defined boundaries for a period of time that may be measured in weeks or months. What's happening here is that enough sellers move in each time at around the high boundary to send the price down again. At the low boundary, enough buyers move in to bounce it back up again. This continues until one side proves stronger than the other. Unlike the head-and-shoulders, this pattern provides no clue to the end of the story. It is only after the price moves decisively out of the rectangle that technical analysts would feel able to call the trend (see Chart X).

Technical analysts and investors who want to get a clearer understanding of trends in individual stocks or market indexes frequently use mathematical techniques to adjust the picture provided by a simple chart showing price and trading volume. One such technique is the moving average. It's used to smooth out the pattern of changing prices in order to get at the longer-term trend, a bit like filtering out the background noise on a telephone line. Plot the moving-average line on the chart and it's possible to compare current prices with the longer-term trend to assess whether it's about to change. A moving average is calculated by adding up the closing prices of a stock or market index for a fixed period of time then dividing the total by the number of prices in that period of time. This is done for each price in succession, but each time the first price in the period is dropped from the calculation and the latest price added. In effect, the calculation moves the average along one unit at a time, from which comes the term "moving average." This effectively slows down the action and makes it easier to see what is happening.

Remember that the principal aim of the technical analyst is to detect whether a price trend has changed direction. A moving average helps because it is designed to lag behind changes in price. If the price trend is up, the moving-average line will show on the chart below the line of current prices. If the price drops through the moving-average line amid heavy trading volume, a technical analyst would see it as a signal to sell. If the previous trend was down, the moving-average line will normally be above current prices. If the price rises through the moving-average line on heavy trading volume, a buy signal would be given (see Chart XI).

Following the moving-average signals faithfully is a good way to avoid big losses. However, this technique will never get you in at the bottom of a price trough or out at the top. Another mathematical tool is the relative strength of a stock when compared with a group of similar stocks or with the market as a whole. The ratio between

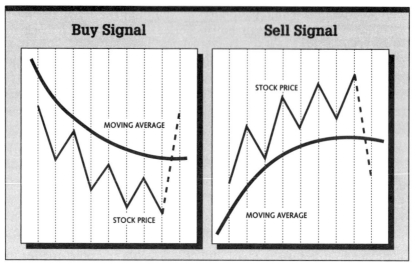

Buy Signal   **Sell Signal**

MOVING AVERAGE

STOCK PRICE

STOCK PRICE

MOVING AVERAGE

CHART XI

Calculating a Five-Week Moving Average

	Closing price
Week 1	$15.25
Week 2	16.50
Week 3	18.00
Week 4	17.35
Week 5	19.25
Total	**86.35**

1. Divide the total of $86.35 by five = $17.27.
2. Plot $17.27 on the chart at end of week 5.
3. At end of week 6, calculate a new five-week total by dropping week 1 ($15.25) and adding week 6's closing price (say, $20.50).
4. Divide the new five-week total ($91.60) by five = $18.32.

TABLE XII

the price in which you are interested and the index you are comparing it with is calculated, and the results plotted on a chart. If the ratio increases, the stock is doing better than the market. It is said to be outperforming the market, and the odds are considered good that it will continue to do so. A stock's relative strength can increase even though its actual price is going down, because the market index is going down faster. Conversely, a falling ratio means the stock is not doing as well as, or underperforming, the market. This, too, can happen even if the actual price is rising, because it's not rising as quickly as the market. Relative-strength ratios are also used to compare the performance of industry groups with the market.

The oldest and most famous pattern said to be revealed by charts of price movements applies only to the movement of the market as a whole, and in particular to the ups and downs of the Dow Jones industrial average. It's called the Dow theory, after its inventor, Charles Henry Dow, who described it in a series of editorials in *The Wall Street Journal* published between 1900 and 1902. Dow was the *Journal's* first editor and the founder of the Dow Jones financial news service. His theory, later elaborated on and formalized by disciples, classifies stock market movements as important primary or major trends, less important secondary or intermediate trends, and minor trends that can be largely ignored. The primary trend is what's meant when analysts and investors say we are in a bull or a bear market. In a bull market, the primary trend is up, and in a bear market the primary trend is down. The key assumption behind the theory is that most stocks follow the underlying market trend most of the time. A second key point is that, although primary trends are interrupted by secondary trends in the opposite direction, they continue for a considerable period of time, usually measured in years. That's why the two-month-long market crash of 1987 was not considered a switch to a primary bear market, even though its size and severity surpassed earlier primary bear markets.

Like other technical theories of market movements, this insight would be of little value to investors unless it offered a way to predict what will happen next. The Dow theory obliges by providing buy signals and sell signals based on the movements of both the Dow Jones industrials average and its associated rails average, transformed since into the transportation average to reflect today's methods of moving goods. Bullish signs are given when the wavelike pattern shown on a chart of these averages indicates that successive rallies are moving to higher peaks and that each intervening decline remains above the previous trough, rather like an incoming tide. Conversely, the reverse pattern indicates the tide is going out and will leave investors high and dry if they aren't careful.

The sensible thought behind the Dow theory is that better times in the economy will be reflected both in the business of the leading industrial companies and in the business of the companies that transport goods, as will poorer times. The theory's most important rule is that the two averages must confirm each other for a valid signal to be given. In today's fast-moving markets, however, this frequently means the Dow theory's signals come too late to be of much help to investors. For instance, after the October, 1987, market crash, the earliest point at which a Dow theorist could call a resumption in the bull market was the following April. By that time, the industrials average had already risen 380 points, or 22 per cent, from its lowest closing value of around 1730 the previous October. Moreover, some Dow theorists would not say that any signal of a resumed bull market was given until mid-1989, when the industrials average was another 200 points higher.

There is no doubt that charting the price and volume history of a stock helps an investor understand the changing supply and demand for the stock in the past. The theories of technical analysis can certainly also help with the timing of buying and selling. There are problems with the approach, though. In hindsight, the patterns drawn by technical analysts on their charts appear self-evident, but by then it's usually too late to take advantage of them. When there is still time to act profitably, while the patterns are still forming, they are by no means so clear. Different technical analysts looking at the same chart often come to quite different conclusions about what will happen.

These problems are worse in today's markets. Technical analysis rests on the belief that the market's movements are related at least partially to such realities as the changing fortunes of companies and of the economy as a whole. But modern computers enable market technicians to call up highly complicated mathematical analyses of the behaviour of prices almost instantaneously. Many of today's professional money managers rely heavily on the signals given by such computer-based analyses, moving hundreds of millions of dollars into or out of the market on their command. More than ever, therefore, the signals become self-fulfilling prophecies and, to that extent, false indicators of the underlying realities. The moral: Use the techniques of technical analysts if they help you to follow what's happened so far, but use them with caution to predict the future.

CHAPTER 10

If It Sounds Too Good to Be True...

THE MOST POPULAR METHOD of picking stocks doesn't employ the fundamental or the technical approaches. Nor does it employ some of the other techniques described later in this book. Instead, it uses what might be called the by-guess-and-by-gossip technique, otherwise known as the hot-tip approach. John Templeton, one of the most successful stock market investors of our time, once described it this way: "Rumours, what other people know, what inside information there is, what the dividends are, who's going to split the stock . . . a sort of haphazard approach."

This was meant as a critical comment, not an endorsement, because this sort of thing can be dangerous to your financial health. The technique is very popular in the later stages of a roaring bull market when the odds of winning are a little better than usual, but not much better. People who normally pay little attention to the stock market begin to hear stories about money being made. They run into people at the office who happily confide the details of their market winnings. "My broker recommended a stock just a month ago and it's doubled since," they hear. Their dinner companions have a tale about a friend who borrowed money to buy a stock he had been tipped about, and who is now considering early retirement on the profits. They ask themselves: How long has this sort of thing been going on? And why are we not getting a piece of this action?

So a new chump is made, to water and fertilize the bull market with money and hope. Chumps are much loved by the less scrupulous sort of broker, and by company managements with an eye to the value of their stock options. Directionless, operating without method or first-hand information, chumps are slaves to the mob psychology that rules the market much of the time.

Let's look at some real-life examples:

Case 1: Is everybody talking about computer stocks going to the moon? Quick, let's buy some. You can't go wrong buying into high-tech, can you? What's that? The stocks are all selling at 50 times earnings, at least? Don't talk to me about price-earnings multiples at a time like this. Are you going to take my order, or not?

Postscript: There was a time when a lot of investors got excited about a Montreal computer company called Comterm. It had developed a personal computer that was going to revolutionize teaching methods in schools, and there was a huge market for the machine. At the peak of the excitement in 1984, the admission price to this action was as high as $13.62 a share. But events did not transpire as predicted because the computer did not work as advertised. Instead of making big profits, the company ran up three years of losses and teetered on the edge of bankruptcy. And the stock? You could buy it for 31 cents at year-end 1989. The company has since gone bankrupt.

Case 2: Is the world running out of oil? Everybody says so. At least, they said so back in the late 1970s. Clearly, you can't go wrong buying a wonderful company like Calgary-based Dome Petroleum. Why, just the other day there was a flattering piece about it in the paper. They've got some really big plans and their top brass are considered very smart. What's that? They haven't actually found any oil in the Arctic and they've taken on some pretty big debts? You're always bothering me with details. Get me 500 shares at the market.

Postscript: In 1981, at their record high of $25.38 (adjusted for a five-for-one stock split that year), 500 shares of Dome Petroleum cost close to $13,000, including commissions. In August, 1988, at their last price of $1.40 on the TSE after the virtually bankrupt company was picked up for a song by Amoco, 500 shares of Dome Petroleum would have brought only $700, less commissions. In January of that year, you would have received less than $1 for each Dome share.

Case 3: Once upon a time, if you were a Quebec taxpayer, you could buy newly printed shares of ambitious young Quebec companies and get $1.50 in tax deductions from the Quebec government for every dollar you laid out. Every deal was a winner and other taxpayers picked up part of the tab. The only problem: getting your broker to set aside some shares for you at the original issue price, before they soared. What's that? The entrepreneurs who are selling a small piece of the company for a lot of money have already raided the store and cleaned out the till? Who's going to buy the shares later on, when the tax break has expired? Why are these people selling shares in their company to the rest of us, anyway? What kind of questions are those? Don't be such a party pooper. You really can't go wrong on a deal like this. The government wouldn't subsidize these investments if they were really risky, would it? Well, yes, it would. In fact, under the rules of the Quebec Stock Savings Plan, the riskier the company, the bigger was the subsidy.

Postscript: There were a handful of long-term winners for investors, but there's a much longer list of bombed-out, forsaken stocks selling at a fraction of what they originally cost. There's also a band of sadder and perhaps even wiser Quebec stock market neophytes who learned the hard way that swinging with the crowd is a dangerous game.

Stock market history is full of such unhappy tales. In the latter part of the 1960s, there was the ill-fated craze for conglomerates. Contemporary business wisdom suggested that managing one company was much the same as managing another, no matter whether they were in steel or cosmetics. So put together a bunch of companies with nothing in common except ownership and top-flight central corporate management, invite investors to buy shares in the company that owns or controls all the others and watch the stock soar. Much money was lost by believers who stayed ardent for too long about such creations.

The start of the 1960s saw a craze for the bowling business. A U.S. stock called Brunswick climbed all the way from nowhere to almost $75 in 1961 on the story that it had an unassailable lock on the business. In the 1962 market crash, it plunged from around $51 to $13.12 at phenomenal speed as investors suddenly saw the story as fiction. In mid-decade, colour television was all the rage and stocks such as Motorola, Admiral, Zenith and Magnavox became the darlings of the crowd. Not long afterward they, too, fell from favour, and their stock prices plummeted.

In the 1920s, Ivar Krueger's International Match Corp. raked in $145 million from investors who bought high-priced new shares of the company. Public belief in the Swedish match king's business genius was so strong that his rickety financial empire even managed to survive the great crash and the start of the Depression. It was not until 1932 that it fell apart and Krueger shot himself. International

Match tumbled into bankruptcy and its stock became all but worthless.

The 18th century saw Britain's South Sea Bubble, a classic tale full of lessons for stock market investors. The South Sea Company was created as a device to raise money from investors to pay off the country's national debt, which had grown enormously as the bills for European wars came in. The company took over three-fifths of the national debt in return for trading privileges and payment to the government of £7 million. The way things were set up, the higher the price that could be obtained for South Sea shares, the less costly the operation would be and the greater the opportunities for the company's managers to profit.

And so it went, helped along by highly effective promotion and a blizzard of hot tips. As some early buyers got out at a profit, later buyers piled in to push the stock up further. By June, 1720, the stock had risen to seven times its price six months earlier. Then the company issued new stock, priced at about eight times the market price six months earlier. What's more, you could buy the shares with a 10 per cent down payment, with the balance paid through instalments over five years. Like many a new issue in later times, this was the peak of the craze and smart investors sold out. As investors cooled on the stock, it began falling just about as quickly as it had risen and by November it was back to where it began the year.

South Sea's rise and fall carried along with it much flotsam and jetsam. At the midsummer peak in the market, hundreds of new schemes were floated. Some of these made a little business sense, but most did not. The ultimate was a notorious company that successfully raised money for the purpose, according to its publicity, of "carrying on an undertaking of great advantage, but nobody to know what it is."

This idea, curiously, was recently revived for a while on the Alberta Stock Exchange in the form of so-called blind pools. This freewheeling exchange allowed promoters to list stock of companies with no assets or business plans. Stock in these Junior Capital Pools, as they were formally known, could originally be sold for as little as five cents each, although the minimum price was later doubled to a dime. The organizers had 18 months to do some sort of business deal with the $50,000 to $100,000 they could raise, if they wanted to make their pool a regularly listed company. Amazingly, there was no shortage of buyers, even though it soon became clear that to some of the promoters, doing a legitimate business deal with the money raised was not the main object.

Clearly, therefore, we are dealing here with something permanent — recurring examples of perverse human behaviour in the stock market that no misfortune seems able to deter. In most fields of endeavour, repeated failure leads to trying something else. The person whose hand-eye coordination and sense of balance are not good enough to avoid frequent falls rarely adopts gymnastics as a lifelong hobby. Yet well-publicized and financially painful reverses suffered in the stock market through following the crowd are constantly succeeded by more of the same.

One reason is that being a chump is more fun than being a loner. New brokers learn quickly that many of their customers are not really in the stock market to make money, although they say they are. Sure, they're happy if they make a bit, but they're also not too unhappy if they lose. What many customers really want is to be part of the action. That's why they flock into the stock market at the worst time, when it's running fast and furious, near the top of a bull market. They want to be able to call their broker and ask how their shares are doing. They want to chat about earnings, takeover rumours, interest rates, the state of the economy, about what's going on. That's also why they can never be persuaded to take an interest early in a bull market, when there's not much action but good deals are to be had.

Brokers also tell tales of customers who use the market as an exercise in masochism. When these doleful types see their winnings snatched in a sudden market storm, the experience appears only to confirm their worst fears about the way the world works. They have done it to me again! Didn't I tell you they would?

Not that there isn't a "they" out there, and what's moving now may indeed be doing so only because "they" are pulling the strings. There are insiders and outsiders in the market. That's why there are insider trading laws designed to give outsiders a better chance at winning. The senior officers of companies with publicly traded stocks are automatically considered insiders of their companies under these rules, as are the directors of such companies and the owners of 10 per cent or more of the shares.

These people are more likely than most to get information that will affect the price of a stock before the rest of the world hears about it. They could, therefore, make big profits from unsuspecting outsiders by trading in the company's shares before general disclosure of the information. The rules generally do not bar such insiders from buying and selling their company's shares. They do have to wait until information that could affect the stock's price has been disclosed publicly. They also have to report their trading later for all to see, especially unhappy outsiders who may sue for recovery of losses sustained from being on the other side of such trades. Many companies also have strict policies restricting trading by employees and directors who acquire undisclosed information likely to affect the price of the stock.

Other people can come into possession of potentially profitable undisclosed information by getting it from insiders. They may be outsiders called in to give professional advice on a takeover, a corporate reorganization, a refinancing, the launch of a new product and so on. They may be investors who receive an advance tip about profitable inside information because of their status or usefulness to the company. Today's insider trading laws attempt to catch such recipients of tips or tippers in their net, but with limited success. It is usually very difficult to prove that a particular transaction was made because of inside information rather than good judgment.

Some cynics say that most stock market transactions happen because someone has inside information. That's why there are customers for investment advice services that keep close tabs on trading reports filed by insiders and recommend copycat transactions. Some investors swear by this technique. Its two main problems are that insiders are not infallible guides even to the fortunes of their own companies and the information is often stale by the time the customers of the advice service get it. In most circumstances company insiders do not have to report their transactions until the tenth day of the following month, and prompt observance of that deadline is neither universal nor enforced effectively.

The cynics' view, like most pessimistic opinions, is exaggerated. But what can be said is that many stock market transactions occur because someone believes they have profitable information not generally available, obtained from somebody thought to be in the know. More often than not, the somebody who was thought to be in the know has obtained the information from someone else believed to be even more in the know. Sometimes the tip may be no more than wishful thinking. Sometimes it may be intelligent anticipation of what's going to happen. Quite frequently, though, the tip is going round because somebody wants it to circulate.

At many companies, investor relations consists only of making sure the company's annual report and periodic financial statements look good and get out on time, having a knowledgeable person available to answer questions from investment analysts and arranging for the boss to speak to groups of analysts from time to time. The closest that such companies come to manipulation of their investment image is to tell the truth loudly when things are going well and to lower the volume a tad when they aren't.

At others, the black art of less scrupulous investor relations is practiced energetically. Earnings news from such companies must be looked at closely to discover the truth. There are some warning signals to look for. The annual report sent to shareholders will usually be primped and gussied up with impressive pictures and equally impressive generalities. Appearances of the company's top brass before groups of investment analysts will be scripted and choreographed with great care and skill. Financial journalists with a record of not probing a company's finances too deeply or skillfully will get full co-operation; their colleagues who prefer to dig hard for a more accurate story will not. Trace an optimistic rumour back far enough and you may find that the executives of such companies and their friends in the investment business are not above starting it in the first place, or at least giving it a helpful nudge.

Investment professionals label such companies "promotional" and remain wary of them. Their carefully painted images may boost the price of their shares for a while, but you had best have your money elsewhere when that image cracks. At such moments, the market behaves like a disillusioned lover who has just discovered his angel has human faults, too. That's frequently when neophyte investors learn that a stock's price can fall farther and faster than it rose.

There are also professional stock promoters. These are people who make a living by buying a cheap, unloved stock, making it loved and expensive, then selling it at a big profit to mesmerized chumps. When the promoter moves out and the price starts to fall, unhappy buyers hunt desperately for somebody to take it off their hands. When the price gets low enough, somebody usually does show up. More often than not, it's the original promoter, sometimes in another guise. A skillful promoter can do this sort of thing repeatedly; buying cheap, marking the stock up and selling out. It's said of the best of the breed that it's a mistake to complain to them in person. You may find yourself sold on a new promotion before you've counted the losses on the previous one.

If you have no strategy for winning in the stock market, you will always be prone to getting caught up in the latest craze and you will always be an easy mark for manipulators. There are three maxims that, if faithfully followed, could help protect you while you are developing and refining your strategy:

• When you hear a hot tip at second- or third-hand — that is, not from your father, the president of the company — always ask yourself: If this is so good, why are they letting me in on it?

• Always ask yourself that question anyway, wherever the tip comes from.

• Remember that if it sounds too good to be true, it probably is.

Read these over several times and commit them to memory. Chanting them at the start of every day the stock market is open might help, too.

CHAPTER 11

Shopping for Value

THERE ARE SEVERAL WAYS to avoid the perils of the hot-tip, follow-the-crowd approach to the stock market. The most effective, if pursued properly, is to buy value. It's rather like never buying anything that isn't on sale. Serious shoppers practice this technique all the time and so can serious stock market investors. True, it's not as much fun as impulse shopping can be, when you buy something just because you feel good and the weather outside is beautiful. And you have to enjoy hunting for a bargain to make it work.

Of course, finding a stock bargain can be tough, just as it is difficult to find the best deals in stores that seem always to be having sales. How do you do it? Much the same way you would shop for anything else, by keeping close track of prices. If an item that sold last week for $49.50 is offered today at $24.95, you may be on to a good thing. Or if an item sells down the street for $100 and in this store at $89.50, you are probably looking at a bargain. Like a good detective, the stock market value hunter must study the clues and weigh the available evidence before reaching a conclusion. It also pays to remember that there are no certainties in bargain hunting, whether it is in stores or in the stock market.

What sort of clues are we talking about? Principally, signs that a company's stock is selling well below its real value. Checking the current stock price is the easy part; the hard part is measuring the company's real value. There are investors and market analysts who argue that the only value that counts is what somebody will pay for the company's stock on any particular day. They say all other values are illusions. Value investors believe, however, that this view is mistaken. They argue that on any given day the prices of many stocks will be nowhere near the real value of the companies that issued them. Some stocks will be vastly overvalued by investors, while others will be equally undervalued. Some will be just about right. Therefore, the odds of success are much better if you sort out which is which, and put your money on the undervalued variety.

There is a second equally important assumption behind value investing: Even though the market is wrong about a stock's value today, it will eventually reach the right conclusion. The ugly duckling will turn into a swan, sooner or later. Other investors will some day pay a reasonable price for the stock, and perhaps more, at which point a value investor will contentedly sell it to them.

Unhappily, this assumption is not always correct. Life is not a fairy tale, and neither is the stock market. Not all ugly ducklings become swans and some stocks remain unloved forever. Curiously, though, the stock market appears to be more romantic than you might expect. Fairy-tale endings occur often enough for value investing to produce rewarding returns.

To improve the odds, value investors take a very conservative approach to valuing a company. They look only at how a company is doing, not at what it may do in the future. In other words, they look at the actual numbers, not the projections. True, it doesn't necessarily follow that a company that has done well in the past will do well in the future, but that's not the point. Value investors do not look at a company's history to judge whether its real value will rise in the future. They look at a company's past and present condition to figure out its value today. Then they check the stock market's valuation of the company, the stock price multiplied by the total number of shares, to see whether it is overvalued, fairly priced or undervalued. It's the same process a potential buyer of the company would go through.

Only companies whose shares emerge from this process clearly undervalued are of interest to a value investor, and the more undervalued the better. Value investors rely on the techniques of fundamental analysis to make evaluations of companies. They concentrate on the numbers in the earnings statement, the balance sheet and the cash flow statement. A frequent starting point is the book value. This is the amount of equity in a company, calculated by subtracting all liabilities and preferred-share amounts from the total assets on the balance sheet. Divide the result by the number of common shares and you get the book value, or equity per share. If the stock price is lower than this, you may have a company worth investigating further. If it's not, move on to the next company.

The mere fact that it sells below book value is not enough to make a stock attractive to value investors. It must pass other tests first. What these investors are looking for is a profitable dividend-paying company that is likely to stay that way because it has a sound business and is not drowning in debt. Yet for one reason or another its stock is available at an attractive price.

The jewel that excites value investors more than anything is a so-called net-net situation. This is a profitable company you can buy for less than the amount of its liquid assets alone — that is, its working capital less all of its liabilities, its intangible assets and its preferred shares at liquidation value. You pay nothing for its ongoing business, land, buildings or equipment. Note that this definition does not include a company that is going bankrupt; they are usually not worth buying at any price.

Are such bargains ever available? Surprisingly, they are. There are more of them in the early stages of a bull market and fewer in the later stages. This fact is another key reason for buying value and not chasing growth. It's remarkable how projections of profit growth become rosier as the price of a company's stock rises. When the techniques of value investing reveal a large number of net-net situations, it's almost certainly late in a bear market or early in a bull market, good times to buy stocks. When there are hardly any such bargains to be found, it's a warning that the party is nearly over. Best not to be still living it up when the bears raid the joint.

You don't have to restrict yourself to such super bargains as net-net situations. Less cheap stocks can also be good buys, so long as they offer good value in relation to their price. The key is always to go through the process of establishing an estimated valuation for a company based on its performance history and current financial state, then check to see that the stock price is below that figure. A minimum one-third discount is a good rule of thumb.

You can hunt for possible bargains in a mechanical sort of way by studying stock guides and company reports. For U.S. stocks, the guides published by Standard & Poor's Corp. and Moody's Investors Service are good sources, as is the Value Line Investment Survey. For Canadian stocks, there are *The Financial Post* surveys and its regularly updated company information service. Computer-savvy investors can now get much of this information electronically, using software that will select only those companies that meet their chosen tests.

Once a likely prospect is found, some value investors go no further, except perhaps to check the annual report for possible surprises or errors by the company-information services. They believe
that the numbers tell the story and that gathering more details will
confuse rather than illuminate. To stay out of trouble with this approach, they buy only stocks that are selling at large discounts and
diversify their holdings among different kinds of companies to less-
en the odds that an unexpected disaster in any one industry will
devastate their portfolio.

However, not all value investors can, or want to, take such an
austere approach. They may not be able to afford more than one or
two stock market investments at a time and they may find doing
everything by the numbers less than enthralling. Having identified a
good prospect, they prefer to find out a lot more about the company
whose stock is being considered. It's amazing how many investors
buy a stock without having a clear understanding of what the company does for a living.

Research of this sort is easier if you already know something
about the business the company is engaged in, perhaps because of
personal experience or the experience of relatives or friends. Try to
find people who know the business, even if they know little about
the company. If you can talk to people who work for its competitors, do so. Act like a reporter assigned to write a profile of the company or a detective checking out its alibi. Most professional
practitioners of value investing try to know as much about a company they invest in as its own management.

There is another important thing to understand about value investing. Coming to conclusions about the real value of a company is
not a cut-and-dried business. What is seen as good value varies from
investor to investor. Value, like beauty, is in the eye of the beholder.
Despite their concentration on the numbers and the facts, value investors practice an art, not a science. A company may be tagged as
cheap, but the trick is to discover whether the stock market actually
knows what it is doing on this one. There may be good reasons for
the stock price to be low, and to go lower still.

Some value investors consider the list of new low prices published in newspapers (the stocks that traded at a record low price that
day), a good source of possible bargains. Most of them will be dogs,
but every now and then diligent research will turn up a potential
winner.

Some value investors look for companies selling cheaply but which have a franchise on their particular business. Franchise has a special connotation here, not its normal meaning of a commercial arrangement. In the world of investment, a company is said to have a franchise on its business if a competitor would find it extremely difficult and expensive to enter the same field. A prime example, well picked over by value investors in the past decade, was the metropolitan daily newspaper. No law prevents the launch of a rival daily, just the economics and business conditions of the trade. Of course, the stock of a company with an impregnable franchise may be too expensive to make it attractive to a value hunter. Also franchises don't always remain impregnable. Metropolitan dailies are not the great businesses they once were.

Some value investors are more finicky still. Even when they have identified a stock selling at well below the real value of the company, they do not invest unless they can also identify a catalyst that will begin the process of closing the gap between the price and the value. This catalyst may be a wave of takeovers of other companies in the same industry. It may be the retirement or death of the principal owner of the company. It may be a company's decision to start buying back its own stock, if the move is based on an informed assessment that the company is worth more than its market price.

Almost all value investors stay well away from a company whose management has a reputation for not being straight with shareholders. It's one thing for the top executives to be enthusiastic and optimistic, but it's quite another thing to be deliberately misleading. Glowing forecasts of sales and profits made at a time when management normally would know better imply dishonesty, or at least incompetence. Constant talk of shrewd acquisitions that never take place is another warning sign. So are repeated predictions that a turnaround in profit is just ahead.

Value investors put more effort than most into deciding what to buy, but that does not exempt them from having to make the difficult decision faced by all stock-market investors: when to sell. However, because a value investor usually has a good understanding of why he or she bought the stock, the technique makes the timing of sales a little easier, at least on paper. If you bought a stock because its market price was well below its real value with a wide margin for error, then surely the time to sell is when that gap disappears. This was, after all, the development you foresaw when others didn't. You can feel happy and content to see your judgment vindicated and to take your well-earned profit from tardy investors who have only just awakened to the real value in the company.

If only it were that simple. There are two problems with that mechanical approach, though. The practical problem is that by not staying aboard for the ride on the winners, you lose the chance of making up for your mistakes on the losers. Inevitably, the prices of some stocks in which you invest will remain cheap forever. Some may even get cheaper as the price falls. The psychological problem is that it is very difficult to part with a stock that has triumphed over all odds. When the world seems finally to be recognizing the value that you spotted much earlier, it seems churlish to walk away from it.

Staying aboard poses more risks, however. You can get caught up in the excitement and forget all about value investing, buying more shares at ever higher prices until suddenly the party is over and you have a big loss instead of the profit you could have taken earlier. You will have to decide for yourself, preferably after personal experience, whether you have the discipline to withstand such temptation. When a stock you bought because it was cheap approaches your estimate of the company's real value, one technique that will avoid some of the risk of staying aboard is to sell enough shares to take out your original stake. Then you have only your profits at risk.

What about the other decision you will have to make — when to sell a cheap stock that stubbornly refuses to become an expensive one? Obviously, if any of the factors on which you based your assessment of a company's real value change for the worse, you should rethink your decision and be prepared to bail out. But if that does not happen, how long should you stay around? Not forever, clearly, but you do have to be patient to practice value investing. A time horizon extending over years, not months, is a necessity. Value investing rests on the usually correct assumption that if you have a rational reason for buying a stock, others will eventually agree with you. But the key word is "eventually." All those other irrational investors out there can be mighty ornery and stupid for a long time. This is the principal reason why value investing will always be a minority sport. Once the excitement of the hunt for a bargain is over, life can get dull while waiting around. The consolation is that the payoffs from successful value investing are more certain and jucier than can be expected from other stock market techniques.

CHAPTER 12

Is Diversification the Answer?

EVEN THE MOST ASTUTE investors pick the wrong stock surprisingly often. John Templeton, a legendary veteran among professional value investors, says he and his competitors get it wrong one time out of three. What chance, then, is there for the rest of us? The best we can reasonably hope for is to be right two-thirds of the time, and most of us won't do even that well. So if we put all our eggs in one basket, the odds that we will lose some of them appear to be unacceptably high.

What's the solution? Templeton and many others recommend spreading your eggs around many different baskets, a technique known as diversification. The idea is that if you buy nine stocks of companies in different industries, and three of them turn out to be dogs because those industries fail to flourish, there's still a good chance the other six will do all right. If, however, you had all your money in one stock in one industry, and that industry happened to be one of the three losers, you are probably going to get hurt badly. It's something like the way insurance companies run their business. By taking premiums from many people, they can pay the few who suffer the misfortunes for which they are insured.

This principle of safety in numbers is the basis of the mutual fund business. Mutual funds consist of large pools of cash collected from customers and invested by professional money managers. The funds may own scores of different stocks, as well as other investments such as bonds or mortgages and varying amounts of cash reserves. You buy units or shares in the fund, which means that you get a small piece of every investment it makes. This ingenious arrangement provides automatic diversification and is especially useful to small-scale investors who would never be able to spread their risks so widely otherwise. Indeed, some investment advisers argue you should always invest in the stock market through a mutual fund unless you are in a position to spread your risks among nine or 10 stocks.

Diversification is certainly a good idea for the majority of stock market investors, most of whom don't have the time, the aptitude or the inclination to master the art of aggressive stock selection. It will almost certainly pay off over the long term for such passive investors, as long as they avoid running with the crowd and getting caught up in the waves of enthusiasm and panic that grip the market from time to time.

There are drawbacks, though. While putting your eggs in many different baskets means you are less likely to lose all of them at once, it also means that you are likely to have at least a few losers most of the time. As a result your gains from winners will be diluted by your losses. The price you pay for greater piece of mind from spreading risk is an investment performance that is more likely to be average than superlative.

This is one reason why the managers of the large pools of money that dominate today's stock market, pension funds, mutual funds and so on, have trouble doing spectacularly better than the market as a whole. The huge amounts in which they deal mean they must use most of the baskets the market offers, most of the time. The ultimate diversified portfolio is one that contains all the stocks in a broad price-measuring index such as the TSE 300 composite index. By definition, of course, such a portfolio cannot do better or worse than the market as a whole. The managers of many large investment funds have, in fact, tried to avoid all their performance problems by buying newly developed products that allow them to invest in the entire index with one order (see Chapter 15).

The second principal drawback has to do with the inevitable limitations of any one investor's knowledge and experience. Nobody can reasonably expect to consistently make more than a handful of brilliant stock selections over a period of time. A serious investor can do enough research and acquire enough knowledge to invest confidently in two or three situations at most, but not in 10 or more. So some market players advise the exact opposite of diversification — concentration. The way to come out ahead, they argue, is to put all your eggs in one or two baskets, and watch those baskets night and day.

The concentration strategy, like value investing, is a minority sport. It should be adopted only by those who are prepared to put in the time needed to learn a lot about picking stocks, and who have the financial resources and psychological fortitude to take the consequences of making a big mistake now and then. There is no doubt that putting everything into a few big winners pays off wonderfully well. But it's a dangerous business.

There are always two decisions to make about a stock. You have to decide when to buy and when to sell, and selling a winner at the right time can be as tough as picking it up in the first place. You can get so pleased with a stock that goes up after you buy it that you fall in love with it. When it stops going up and starts going down, you feel that the market is treating your loved one badly, and maybe you buy some more just to even the score. From there, it's a short step to following it all the way down, giving up all your profits and maybe some of your original investment as well.

The safer and less-wearing strategy of diversification can be carried out in the stock market in several different ways. A popular way is to spread your investments among companies in a range of industries. Maybe you buy a bank stock, a mining stock, a food stock and a telephone utility, plus something in forest products, oil and gas, communications, steel and real estate. The TSE 300 index gives you a dozen or so major industries to choose from, most of them subdivided into additional categories.

To make this work, you should include in your list industries that prosper in different business conditions. For example, when the economy is just chugging along and interest rates are falling, the bank stock and the utility stock should do well. They are popular among investors who want a steady flow of income because their generous and reasonably safe dividend payments become more attractive as the interest available on competing securities such as bonds and term deposits shrinks. But such times are not as good for natural resource stocks, so your mining and forest-products investments will probably languish. They will find their place in the sun when the economy is straining at the seams and the demand for metals and timber is soaring. In turn, the food stock and the utility stock will probably find favour as a defensive investment when the economy is in a recession or when a majority of investors believe a recession is around the corner.

You can spread your investments among broad sectors of the economy, putting some in industries especially sensitive to the rise and fall of interest rates such as real estate, some in regulated industries that can raise their prices to cover rising costs in good times and bad, some in basic industries such as steel and some in consumer products industries such as brewing.

Another way to diversify is by geographical location. In Canada, the economies of the industrial heartland of Ontario and Quebec and of the resource-rich West move in different cycles. It is possible for Central Canada to be booming and for the West to be just getting by. For much of the 1980s this was the case. Yet in the second half of the 1970s, soaring prices for oil and gas produced a roaring boom in the West on a scale to make Central Canadians envious. Again, the successive rise and fall of separatism in Quebec has had an impact on investment returns in that province from time to time and will probably do so again.

You can also diversify your investments among companies in different countries. Investing near home makes sense because it is usually easier to keep track of what is going on, but it's a good idea to hedge your bets on Canada. An investment or two in U.S., British or Japanese stocks could help if Canada's budget problems lead to a major crisis of confidence in the country's economic management. It's not only that you may find a good bargain or two outside Canada; you may receive your winnings in a currency that is worth more in Canadian dollars than when you made the initial investment.

Choosing investments with differing degrees of risk is another approach. Part of your portfolio could be in conservative low-risk stocks of companies with histories of steady profits and dividends in good times and bad. Another portion could be in growth stocks, companies with a record of fast-rising sales and profits and a good chance of a continuing high growth rate. Depending on your financial circumstances and your tolerance for risk, a third portion might go into a venture-type investment. This would be the stock of a company that is pioneering new products or services in a fast-changing industry. Today, the computer and electronics industries are prime examples. Many companies flock to such industries because of the possibility of explosive growth and a cascade of profits, but only a few survive the inevitable shakeouts. Choosing the few is a tricky business, but it pays off well if you get it right.

Finally, you might try to spice up your portfolio, and probably raise your anxiety level, with an outright speculation or two, but only with money you can afford to lose. The term "speculative" is frequently reserved for the stocks of companies engaged on a small scale in looking for metals, minerals or oil and gas. These exploration company shares are called penny stocks because their prices are usually quoted in cents instead of dollars, and buying and selling them should not be confused with investing.

But the shares of other kinds of companies, including large and long-established outfits, can also be considered speculative from time to time. Buying the shares of a company because it may be taken over at a higher price is speculation. Buying the shares of a company in deep financial trouble on the possibility of a turnaround is also a speculation. So is buying the shares of a growth company whose stock has risen so far that the price discounts the next century, rather than just the next five years' earnings. Uninformed enthusiasm may carry the price higher still, but the odds are not good enough to bet your last dollar on it.

CHAPTER 13

Playing the Takeover Game

TAKEOVERS, ESPECIALLY WHEN contested, are the earthquakes of the corporate world. They radically change the contours of a familiar landscape, shake people loose from what once appeared to be lifetime attachments, divert and sometimes stunt executive careers, cost employees their jobs and lay bare the inner workings of companies to intense public scrutiny. In the stress of corporate combat, normally cool and rational business leaders behave emotionally, even passionately. They scratch and hiss like alley cats. In defence of their territory, they spend the company's money copiously on costly mercenaries to engage the raiders; lawyers, investment experts, public relations advisers. They publicly embrace principles of corporate morality, if that seems likely to help. Simultaneously, they may launch sharp-practice schemes that barely stay on the right side of the law, and sometimes don't. For the onlooker, it all makes for great stories, which is why takeovers receive more press coverage than most other business news. And for investors not personally affected by the fallout of a bitter power struggle, takeovers provide some of the best opportunities for big profits.

Reaping those profits can be, of course, a stressful business. For example, until the final hours of the 1989 battle for ownership of the Montreal-based supermarket chain, Steinberg Inc., it was not clear which was the best way for outside investors to jump. In another recent bid, investors in the real estate arm of the parent company of Bell Canada had to make a difficult decision: Was it better to accept an admittedly low-ball offer from the Reichmann brothers or hang on and risk never seeing that price again. Most did not accept, the Reichmanns walked away and the real estate company's shares afterward became worth next to nothing. This is not a game for people who want to put their money away in something safe and collect dividend cheques without paying much attention.

The profit opportunity in takeovers is a consequence of their nature. No company takeover is likely to succeed if the bidder does not offer more for its shares than the previous market price. Normally, the market price of a reasonably well-traded exchange-listed stock discounts all that is generally known about the company's value and business prospects. A takeover bidder figures, however, that there is additional value in the company that is not being recognized by investors. In the Steinberg struggle, for instance, the rival bidders believed that the company's large property holdings were overshadowed in investors' minds by its supermarket business, which was not doing well. As a result, the company could be bought at a price that would be attractive to existing shareholders. It could then be split up and its parts sold for more than was paid for the whole.

There is a host of other reasons why a takeover bidder is prepared to pay a premium over the going market price of a company's shares. A company may be more valuable to a particular bidder for business reasons. The bidder may be in a similar line of business and see an opportunity to expand by buying additional existing production capacity rather than building it from scratch. Similarly, the bidder may see an opportunity to expand a sales distribution network, to acquire a promising product or even to remove a competitor from the arena. A bidder may judge that a company's management has lost its edge and is no longer exploiting the assets effectively, and these failings have depressed its stock price. There may even be a pile of cash in the company treasury awaiting more imaginative use. Move in and change the management, make profitable use of the cash, and the stock price can be expected to recover smartly and reward the bidder. Sometimes a bidder may see a once-in-a-lifetime chance to acquire a coveted company that was previously under firm family control but is now plagued by family conflicts that make it vulnerable to raiders.

It's important to realize that some takeover bids occur because there are corporate empire builders who are happiest when buying and selling companies. Such people are bored and frequently not very good at the slow business of nurturing companies through the ups and downs of business cycles, installing high-quality management and supporting long-term policies aimed at survival and growth. They are good at, and excited by, the cut and thrust of deal-making and raiding. As a result, not all takeover bids make rational business sense, as the rise and subsequent fall of some builders of shaky empires shows. The unhappy ending to Canadian financier Robert Campeau's foray into the U.S. retail business is a good example. So is the Steinberg takeover, as it happens. It turned out badly for the winner and the company.

For investors, the takeover game has two phases: You can play before a takeover bid is launched, or after. The first phase calls for you to spot likely takeover targets in advance. You do this by thinking about companies the way a potential bidder thinks about them. You look for situations such as Southam Inc., the Canadian publishing company controlled and run from its creation by members of the Southam family.

In the last decade, investors came to the conclusion that Southam's management was falling behind its rivals in adapting to the changing business environment. So its stock price lagged behind. In 1985, the sudden death of the company's chief executive helped focus attention on it as a possible takeover target. A subsequent anti-takeover deal with a friendly newspaper publisher, Torstar Corp., led to some violent swings in investor opinion of management and the stock. That year the price swung between a low of $12.12 and a high in late summer of $17.87, as takeover rumours flourished. Since then, the stock has never been below $12.25 and it traded at more than twice that level for most of 1989.

Buying early and hanging on until mid-1990 would have paid off well. Nimble trading could also have brought dramatic results. During January, 1988, Southam shares traded at about $16.50, but less than 12 months later they had risen all the way to a high for the year of $32. Buyers in early January who sold in December near the year's high would have almost doubled their money. Over that period the company's operating performance did not improve at all, although its management was credited with laying the groundwork for later improvements. The principal reason for the gain in the stock price was the prospect that an outside bidder would pay a big premium to acquire Southam.

The long courtship and eventual stormy conquest of Falconbridge Ltd. by Noranda Inc. provides a typical example of the opportunities and perils of the second phase. Noranda, one of Canada's biggest mining companies, had had its eye on Falconbridge for a long time. What it wanted, in particular, was its target's rich Kidd Creek mine in Ontario.

Falconbridge was also big, a leading Canadian producer of nickel and copper. Early in 1988, its stock was oscillating between $21 and $24, although it briefly dipped below $20. By midsummer, it had climbed to as high as $28 in sustained heavy trading. The climb was accompanied by big price swings. By August, though, it settled back more or less to where it started the year. Then later that month Noranda revealed publicly that it had built up a stake of just under 20 per cent of the company through purchases of shares on the market. Its average cost was $22.50 a share. The stake was an investment, Noranda said, and it had no plans to acquire more.

These developments provided further evidence that Noranda had more than a passing interest in Falconbridge and at some time might well make a bid for the whole company. No doubt some far-sighted investors took note of this and tucked the stock away in anticipation of such a move. However, most did not. There was enough uncertainty about Noranda's intentions to make many people shy away from placing a bet at that point. Even when Noranda announced at the end of September that it was planning an offer through stock exchanges for another 10 per cent of the company at $22.25 a share, the stock did not take wing. It languished in the general area of that price until late November.

Meanwhile, government regulators blocked Noranda's planned stock exchange bid because of a breach of rules, to which the company responded by giving notice it might return to open-market buying to get the shares. That notice was renewed the following May but it was not until June that the company announced it had added a big block of shares to its previous purchases and achieved its objective. The price of the block: $32. Looking at trading records between December and the following June, it is clear that Noranda was picking up shares throughout the period but that the market price had shown signs of running away on the buyer. By early January, the stock had risen to close to $29. It went through $30 by March, $31 in April and $32 in May. During this period, it became clear to anybody who was paying attention that Noranda was attempting a creeping takeover of Falconbridge. As things turned out, anybody who bought stock during that period could eventually have got out at a profit.

Not that things were as cut and dried as they appear in hindsight. Noranda chose its stealthy behind-the-scenes strategy to avoid the cost of taking the target by storm in a frontal attack. It hoped to win without attracting rival bidders who might make the acquisition ruinously expensive, and it might well have got away with it. If so, buying into the game at the prices of early spring would probably not have been too rewarding. Noranda might have accumulated just 51 per cent, enough to ensure control, then stopped and allowed the price to fall again. Alternatively, it might have gone to two-thirds, enough to push through a corporate reorganization, then done the same thing.

None of this happened, though. In early August, a rival bidder appeared. With the stock back below $30, a U.S. mining giant, Amax Inc., launched an offer for all Falconbridge shares at $36.12 each. In one day, the stock jumped more than $6 to $36.62, a 20 per cent gain. Why did the price rise above the Amax offer? Because investors figured Noranda would not back off without a fight. This assessment was correct. Less than two weeks later, Noranda revealed it had lined up an ally, a Swedish industrial group called Trelleborg AB. Their joint bid topped the bid from Amax, but by only a small amount. They offered $37 a share.

Now the attention turned to Amax. Companies frequently make opening takeover bids that are less than they are prepared to pay if necessary. Surely the U.S. company would come back with a higher offer and the bidding auction would continue. Many investors backed this assessment with big orders for Falconbridge stock and the price soared to $39. These purchases turned out not to be the smartest of moves. Amax's first offer proved to be its last. After pondering its response for the rest of August, the U.S. company announced it was pulling out of the fight. The Noranda-Trelleborg bid of $37 a share remained the only offer on the table.

What are the lessons to be learned from a study of the Falconbridge takeover saga? Again, thinking like a bidder and getting into the game early in 1988 would have paid off handsomely. Patience and a willingness to take the risk that Noranda would get its prize without having to pay a high takeover premium to all other shareholders was necessary, however.

Faster profits would have come from nimble footwork as Noranda closed in on Falconbridge in mid-1989. You could have bought the stock at around $30 and seen it jump all the way to $39 as Amax made its play. Buying in at more than the Amax bid price clearly would have been a mistake. Still, you can hardly blame the people who did it because betting on a costly auction between the rival bidders has worked well in similar situations. It just doesn't work every time, which is why you should play the second-phase game only with money you can afford to lose.

Takeover sprees come in cycles, too. In the early stages, the bidders are able to conquer their targets while paying reasonable prices for shares. Later, the prices of attractive targets become steeper. Frequently, the bids can be paid for only on the basis either of getting 100 per cent and gaining access to the cash flow of the target company afterwards, or of selling off parts of it to raise cash, or sometimes both.

This development provides another way to play the takeover market. If a potential target has subsidiary companies with stocks listed on an exchange, you can buy them instead of the parent company. You can win two ways. The successful bidder may have to pay high prices to collect 100 per cent of the subsidiaries' shares in order to get at their cash flow without the complications of dealing with minority shareholders. Alternatively, those subsidiaries may be auctioned off at premium prices.

CHAPTER 14

The Dangerous Magic of Leverage

ARCHIMEDES, THE EARLY Greek thinker with a feel for a vivid phrase, wrote this glowing tribute to the lever: "Give me where to stand, and I will move the earth." He was talking about the mechanical principle with which any 90-pound weakling can lift a one-ton car to change a wheel, so long as he has a jack and a firm piece of ground to stand it on. The jack, which is merely a sophisticated sort of lever, magnifies the physical strength of the stranded driver manyfold, as does the wrench he uses to remove the wheel nuts. And the job is done, with the aid of leverage and without the aid of Superman.

Leverage also works in the world of finance and investment. By using it you can make one dollar do the work of many. If all goes well, you will magnify your profits dramatically. Many of the stock market's big winners use leverage boldly and effectively. But be warned from the start: Leverage is double-edged. If things go wrong when you are using it, your losses will be magnified dramatically, too, just as a car that slips off a jack can kill a careless driver trapped under it. Most of the really big losses in the stock market result from leveraged investments that turn sour.

Financial leverage works this way: Suppose you find an investment that offers a safe 10 per cent return. Put $1,000 of your savings into it and 12 months later you will have $100 in profit, plus your original $1,000, for a total of $1,100. Now suppose you had been able to borrow $9,000 from a friend, interest-free, so that you invest $10,000 instead of $1,000. At the end of 12 months you would have $1,000 in profit instead of $100, plus the borrowed $9,000 and your original $1,000, for a total of $11,000. You could pay back the $9,000 and emerge from the deal with your original stake doubled. Even if your friend charged you 9 per cent interest on the loan, you would still come out ahead. Your profit in that case would be $190, nearly double the profit made without using leverage. As long as your borrowing cost is less than the return on the investment, and as long as you get back all the money you invested, using somebody else's funds to leverage your investment will magnify your winnings.

But take careful note of the word "safe." If you put your money into Canada Savings Bonds or bank term deposits, you get a fixed rate of return and the promise that you will get back all of your original investment on the due date. Although the stock market offers the prospect of dazzling gains, it offers no such guarantees. Dividend payments do increase as companies make bigger profits, giving you a rising return on your investment, and share prices do rise so that you get back much more than you laid out when you cash in. That's not always what happens, though. Always remember that investing in the stock market is a risky business. Dividend payments can be cut or even eliminated as companies struggle with business reverses, and share prices can fall.

Suppose your $1,000 was invested in 100 shares of a $10 stock and soon afterward the company stopped paying dividends. After dropping sharply in price, the stock recovers and you get out a year later at $9. You've lost 10 per cent of what you invested, plus commissions and the interest you could have earned on your $1,000 if you had left it in the bank. That's not good, but it's not a disaster. You've still got $900 to play with and maybe the next stock you buy will be a winner. But suppose you had leveraged this investment by borrowing $9,000 and buying 1,000 shares. If you get out at $9, you can repay the loan, but you will be out the commissions and the interest. Much worse, all your original stake is lost. A 100 per cent loss of your capital was not exactly what you had in mind when you ventured into the stock market.

Now suppose you got out at $8, not $9. Where would you be? That's right, not only would you have lost your original $1,000 and be out the commissions and the interest, you would have only $8,000 to repay a $9,000 loan. So you would have to dip into your savings for another $1,000. To call this a disaster would not be an exaggeration, and it's the kind of thing the stock exchanges were thinking about when they established rules designed to prevent foolhardy customers from heavily leveraging their investments.

Not that the exchanges want to dissuade investors from using leverage. Far from it; buying stocks partly with borrowed money is built into the system. Most brokerage firms offer their customers two ways to invest. Those with cash accounts are expected to pay the full cost of their purchases by a specified settlement date, usually three business days after the order was executed. Cash customers are also expected to deliver to their broker within the same period any shares they have sold. In contrast, customers with margin accounts are allowed to pay only a portion of the full cost of a purchase and borrow the rest of the money from the firm, paying interest at the going rate. You should note that you must always have enough money or investments in a margin account to meet the margin requirements for a transaction. The arrangement is not quite the same thing as a credit card account. But margin accounts do enable you to leverage your investments effectively and conveniently.

Margin refers to the proportion of the price that the customer provides personally. Stock exchange rules oblige member firms to require their customers to pay fixed minimum amounts, depending on the kinds of stock being bought and their market price. These minimums are raised and lowered by the exchanges from time to time. The idea is to allow the widespread use of leverage while keeping it from getting out of hand. In speculative markets, customers will be required to pay more. In tranquil conditions, they will be required to pay less. In mid-1996, for example, typical minimum margin requirements ranged from 30 per cent of the market price to 80 per cent. Brokers were allowed to lend up to 70 per cent of the purchase price of stocks listed on a Canadian exchange that were selling for $5 or more and which met other tests related to options trading. Smaller loans were permitted on lower-priced stocks, down to 20 per cent on those selling for $1.50 to $1.74. Stocks trading below that price could not be bought on margin. A limited number of stocks not listed on a recognized stock exchange also qualify for margin purchases under the same restrictions, although most do not. Note that many firms have a policy of requiring more than the minimum margin prescribed by stock exchange rules.

These minimum requirements apply at the time of the original transaction, but the catch is that they change in line with the market price of the shares bought on margin. If the price goes up, there is no problem. But if it goes down, the minimum amount the customer has to provide goes up. Here is an example of how you can be caught out this way.

You buy 1,000 shares of a listed stock on margin at $2 a share, on which 50 per cent margin is required:

Total cost of the purchase (excluding commission)	$2,000
Broker's maximum loan (50% of $2 x 1,000)	−$1,000
Margin put up by you (50% of $2 x 1,000)	$1,000
The market price of the shares drops sharply to $1.70, where 80% margin is required:	
Original cost of the purchase (excluding commission)	$2,000
Broker's maximum loan (20% of $1.70 x 1,000)	$ 340
Gross margin requirement	$1,660
Original margin deposit	−$1,000
Net margin deficiency	$ 660

Your broker sends you a polite letter informing you that your account is undermargined by $660 and asking you to put things right, either with a cheque for that amount, with investments that have a sufficient value, or with instructions to sell the shares or other securities. However, if the broker sees this as an emergency situation, you may be telephoned.

This request is known as a margin call, and however velvet-gloved its tone, there is an iron fist behind it. That's because to open a margin account you have to sign a margin agreement that puts all the weapons in your broker's hands. In particular, the agreement authorizes your broker to sell undermargined shares at the going market price without telling you in advance. Brokers usually do not sell you out without notice, realizing that this is not good for customer relations. But if a stock you bought on margin is falling far and fast, or in the frenzy of a general market crash, it may happen to you.

Should you ever pay up on a margin call? Probably not. It's too much like throwing good money after bad. There are many market experts who say that if an investment has gone so far wrong that a margin call is made, it's better to let yourself be sold out and move on to something else. Yet it may not be easy to follow this good advice because it involves the psychological difficulty of recognizing that you have made a mistake that is costing you money.

You will avoid this uncomfortable dilemma most of the time by being cautious with your margin account. If you always provide more than the minimum margin required, you will have a shock absorber to protect against margin calls triggered by modest price changes. Extra money or valuable investments in your account will also reduce the likelihood of being sold out willy-nilly as a result of violent price swings. But remember that a margin agreement usually gives your broker the right to sell not just the shares that are under-margined, but any and all of the shares or other investments held in your account. While you owe money to your broker, those shares and other investments can also usually be pledged as security by the broker for general business loans. They can also usually be lent to the firm or to other customers without restriction. What's more, any money in your account is not kept segregated by the brokerage firm, which can use it for its own general business purposes. If the firm gets into financial trouble, you are just another creditor, al-though an industry-supported fund has so far successfully bailed out customers caught in such difficulties. So it's also a good idea not to provide too fat a cushion in your margin account.

Of course, you don't have to borrow from your broker to leverage your stock market investments. You can pay full price and borrow part or all of the money elsewhere. Personal credit lines at your bank or trust company are convenient but expensive sources. If your credit is good, you will probably be able to borrow more cheaply by pledging the purchased shares as security for the loan. However, if the market price of the shares falls, you will almost certainly be asked to put up more money or additional security. Failing that, you will be sold out in similar fashion to a margin account. Family or friends may also be sources of borrowed money for leveraged in-vestments, especially if you can demonstrate a talent for winning in the market. Remember, however, that this must be done informally and not as a business. You usually need qualifications and a licence to set up as a professional money manager.

From time to time, companies provide their shareholders and other investors with a special kind of investment that employs a high degree of leverage. It's known as a warrant and it usually gives whoever owns it the right to buy new common shares from the com-pany at a fixed price for a fixed period of time, normally a year or more. There are also warrants that give owners the right to buy something else at a fixed price — a company bond, perhaps, or a commodity such as gold. Warrants are frequently offered along with initial sales of bonds or preferred shares to help sell the new securi-ties to investors. Later, if they are exercised, they will be a source of equity capital for the company.

Warrants are traded separately, just like stocks, after they are de-tached from the newly issued securities, which may take place im-mediately or after a stipulated period of time. The fixed price at which the common shares can be bought is known as the warrant's exercise price. It is always set higher than the market price of the stock at the time the warrant is created. Otherwise, the warrant would almost certainly be exercised right away, which is not what the company has in mind. If and when the market price of the stock rises above the exercise price, the warrant acquires what is known as an intrinsic value. For example, a warrant that can be used to buy a stock at $20 when the market price of the stock is $25 has an intrinsic value of $5.

Interestingly, warrants usually have a market value even when the market price of the stock is below the exercise price and there is no intrinsic value. This results from the so-called time value of the warrant, which reflects the chance that it will acquire an intrinsic value before it expires. This time value diminishes as the warrant's expiry date approaches and it becomes zero when the warrant expires. For similar reasons, the warrant's market price will frequently reflect what's known as overvaluation. You may see a warrant exercisable at $12 per share trading in the stock market for $1.50 at a time when the market price of the stock is just $10. To buy the stock indirectly through the warrant would cost you $1.50 plus $12, for a total of $13.50. Yet you can buy the stock direct for $10. The $3.50 difference is the overvaluation.

Why would anyone buy the warrant in such circumstances? The main reason is the prospect of using leverage. It costs much less right now to buy the warrant than the stock, and if the stock rises to, say, $15 before the warrant expires, you will do much better than buying the stock directly. Here are the numbers (ignoring commissions):

Cost of 100 shares at $10	$1,000
Sell 100 shares later at $15	$1,500
——Profit	$ 500
——Percentage gain	50%
Cost of 100 warrants at $1.50	$ 150
Sell 100 warrants when stock is $15	
(minimum price based on intrinsic value of $3)	$ 300
——Profit	$ 150
——Percentage gain	100%

Remember, as always, that leverage can work the other way around and hurt you badly. If a warrant is worthless when it expires, which many are, you lose 100 per cent of your investment.

The comfort is that you have a much smaller amount of capital at risk than if you had bought the stock. Warrants also offer you a way of fixing the cost of a stock you really want to buy but can't afford right now.

Another way in which a new issue of company shares is sometimes made more attractive is through an instalment-payment plan. The full price of the shares on offer may be $10, for example, but buyers have to pay perhaps $6 to begin with. The balance of $4 may then be payable a year later. Some issues have been sold with a three-instalment schedule.

Going this route, a buyer acquires what's known as an instalment receipt. These are bought and sold on a stock exchange just like ordinary common shares. But the leverage effect of putting up only part of the price produces larger swings in the receipt price—both up and down. In addition, the owner of the receipt still usually gets a full dividend payment, which raises the yield on the initial investment dramatically.

There is still another, little-understood form of leveraged stock market investment called selling short. It's difficult to follow when first encountered and many people consider it unsporting, but it is an essential feature of the market. Most people are familiar with and see nothing wrong with profiting from a rise in the market price of a stock, even though that profit may be made at the expense of somebody else. But the idea of profiting from a drop in the market price of a stock is less familiar. Inherently, there is no difference, however. If you can buy a stock at $5 and sell it to somebody else for $10, pocketing the gain, why should you not be able first to sell a stock to somebody else for $10, take the chance of being able to buy it back for only $5, and pocket the profit if the deal works out? You would engage in this practice of selling short only if you believe the stock's price is about to fall. But this is merely the mirror image of buying a stock because you believe its price is going up.

The problem in understanding this technique is to accept that it is possible to sell something you don't own. In most circles and in most circumstances, that would be illegal as well as unacceptable. In the stock market, it's perfectly legal as long as you abide by the rules. What you do is have your broker borrow the stock you want to sell short, frequently from another customer's margin account. The stock is then sold at the going market price and, if all goes well, you buy it back later at a lower price and return it to its rightful owner. This is known as covering your short. Any cash that remains in the margin account after the buyback belongs to you. And if the stock goes up instead of down? You may decide to buy it at the higher price anyway and pay out on your losses, or your broker may do that for you, whether you want to or not.

Clearly, this is a tricky business. If you buy a stock at $5, the most you can lose is $5 plus commissions. Your maximum loss is 100 per cent of the capital you risked. However, if you sell a stock short at $5 and it goes into orbit, your loss is theoretically infinite. In practice, you would be sold out pretty quickly, but you can easily lose more than 100 per cent of the capital you risked, especially if you throw good money after bad.

Stock exchanges are as aware of this as you should be. That's why the rules say there must always be a credit balance in a short seller's margin account that exceeds the market value of the shares sold short by fixed percentage amounts. Like the regular margin requirements, these percentages vary from time to time and according to the price and type of shares involved. In recent times they varied from 130 per cent of the market value for listed shares selling at $5 or more and eligible for options trading to 100 per cent plus 25 cents a share for listed shares selling for less than 25 cents. The same limited group of unlisted shares specified under regular margin rules is subject to these short-sale margin requirements. But at the time of writing it was also possible at some firms to sell short other unlisted stocks under stringent margin requirements: 200 per cent of the market price on shares selling for 50 cents or more and 100 per cent of the market price on shares selling for less than 50 cents.

Again, these requirements are based on the market price of the stock at the time of the original short sale, but are adjusted as the price changes. If it moves against you, that is up instead of down in the case of a short sale, the amount of margin required increases. Without an adequate cushion of excess money or other investments in your account, you may face a margin call. Here is how it works if you sell short 100 shares of a listed stock at $25, on which 150 per cent margin is required:

Minimum account balance required (150% of $25 x 100)	$3,750
Proceeds of short sale (excluding commission)	−$2,500
Minimum margin required	$1,250

1. The stock price drops to $15 and you decide to cover and happily take your profit.

Money and credit in your account	$3,750
Cost of buying stock in market (excluding commission)	−$1,500
Your original margin deposit	−$1,250
Pretax profit on short sale	$1,000

2. The stock price rises to $30 and you decide to cover the short and take your loss.

Minimum account balance required (150% of $30 x 100)	$4,500
Proceeds from short sale (excluding commission)	−$2,500
Margin required now	$2,000
Original margin deposit	−$1,250
Margin deficiency (amount of margin call)	$ 750

Cost to buy shares in market	$3,000
Proceeds from short sale (excluding commission)	−$2,500
Pretax loss on short sale	$ 500

There is no prescribed limit on how long you can wait before covering a short sale, but several things can happen to make up your mind for you. If the price moves against you, the amount of margin you have to put up will increase and at some point — preferably early, rather than later — you may decide the game is no longer worth it. Your broker may also find it impossible to borrow replacement stock for you. If so, you are required to buy the shares and cover the short sale, whatever the market price may be. This sort of problem occurs most often in short sales of a stock in which there is not normally much trading volume. That makes it a good idea to restrict your short selling to companies with a large number of shares trading in the market and which are held by many shareholders.

It is illegal under securities law not to tell your broker that you do not own the shares you want to sell, in other words, not to declare that it is a short sale. Your broker is required to make reasonable efforts to find out whether you are breaking that rule. The stock exchanges also have trading rules that restrict short sales at a price below the price of the last previous sale. These are designed to stop a cascade of short sales from producing a runaway collapse in prices. In addition, exchanges publish reports of total short posi-tions in listed shares: twice a month in the case of Toronto, Mont-real and Alberta, and weekly for Vancouver.

Is short selling a game for you? It can pay off handsomely if you get it right. Some noted figures in stock market history made a lot of money that way. But it poses considerable practical and psychologi-cal problems. There is the need to find stock to borrow and to meet margin requirements. A short seller is also responsible for any divi-dends or other benefits paid by the company during the period be-fore the sale is covered. The buy-in rules are an ever-present threat. So is the possibility of being caught in what's called a short squeeze, which is not as much fun as it sounds. This happens if an unexpected price rise stampedes short sellers into trying to cover their sales at the same time and at any price. Up-to-date information on the size of short positions in a stock is not easily available. There are no daily reports from the exchanges and no data at all for un-listed stocks.

Above all, there is the psychological problem to overcome. Most people feel more comfortable profiting from winners than from los-ers, and the stock market reflects that fact of human nature. A happy crowd of optimists is good for business because trading vol-umes generally rise as stock prices rise. An unhappy, pessimistic crowd is not; trading slumps and brokers get fired. The whole in-vestment business is geared mostly to finding and publicizing stocks that are going up, not down. Your average broker has a long list of buy recommendations easily available. Lists of good short sales are brief or don't exist at all. You will usually have to find good candidates yourself, and that can be a lonely business.

Of course, the opportunity to do well by selling short is created by these difficulties. Long lists of good stocks to buy are all very well, but you will frequently find that the price has already gone up to reflect the company's exciting prospects before you hear the story. The competition for good stocks to buy at bargain prices is fierce. The competition for good short sales is usually not. If you can keep a cool head amid the uncritical optimists, you can win at this game.

CHAPTER 15

The Strange World of Futures and Options

PICKING A STOCK YOU THINK will go up is mostly what stock market investing is about. But it is also possible to back your opinion of the outlook for the market without ever taking the additional risk of choosing particular stocks from the rest of the herd.

One way is to buy TIPs, short for Toronto 35 index participation units. These are units in a trust designed to track accurately the ups and downs in the TSE 35 index. In effect, a representative selection of stocks included in the index are put away in a drawer and tickets to play are sold. TIPs trade on the TSE like stocks, pay dividends quarterly and are eligible for registered retirement savings plans.

Buy some and you will get a stake in a representative selection of big-company stocks of all varieties. It's an excellent method of diversifying your stock market investment with only a small amount of money available. You will find TIPs listed under that name among the regular stock quotes. In mid-1996, they were changing hands at roughly $27 apiece. For perhaps $2,700, plus commissions, you in effect acquired a small portfolio invested 17 per cent in banks, 19 per cent in mining companies, 9 per cent in utilities such as the telephone company, 16 per cent in companies that make industrial products, 8 per cent in consumer products companies and the rest scattered among most other kinds of businesses. To diversify a portfolio similarly, using individual stocks, would cost a great deal more money.

Investing in TIPs is rather like investing on auto pilot. You will never do better than the stocks of the leading blue chip companies in the Canadian market do, on average. Pick stocks smartly yourself and you can improve on that. But a TIPs investment does guarantee you will not do worse than those blue chips either, although these big-company stocks do lag behind the rest of the market from time to time. Many investors, amateur or professional, would be content with that.

Two other devices you can choose from are stock index options and stock index futures. However, until and unless you become a big-time, experienced and probably professional player, you should stick to options and stay away from futures. That's because the most you can lose from buying an option is the money you pay for it. With a futures contract, you can lose that amount and much more.

Index options are a recently introduced variation on an old stock market theme. Options on shares have been around since the early days of stock markets, although it is only during the last two decades that exchanges have made it easy to buy and sell them. An option is a contract that gives its owner the legal right to buy or sell something at a fixed price within a certain period of time. The key difference between it and a futures contract is that the owner of an option has no obligation to buy or sell anything. As the saying goes, it's entirely optional. If the owner chooses not to exercise the right to buy or sell provided by the contract, the option expires and the contract is void. The owner of a futures contract, however, takes on a legal obligation to buy or sell something on a fixed date in the future. Most futures players pass this obligation on to somebody else by selling their contracts before that date. But if for some reason they can't do that, they have to meet their obligations one way or another.

Given the difficulties and complexities of buying and selling the stocks themselves, why is anybody interested in taking on the additional complications and risks of options or futures? It's because these devices provide formidable amounts of leverage. For a fairly small admission ticket, you get to play with a big stake. In mid-1996, for instance, you could buy a call option on 100 shares of the Bank of Montreal for a dollar a share, about 3 per cent of the full price of the shares. If you choose right, the rewards are greatly magnified. Conversely, as with all forms of financial leverage, your losses as a result of choosing wrong are equally magnified. However, the key benefit of options is that your maximum loss is fixed in advance. For individuals who want to speculate in fast-moving volatile stocks, they are a good choice.

A stock option may give you the right to buy the underlying stock. In that case, it is described as a call option because you can call the stock away from the option seller at the agreed price, known

Canadian equity options

Stock Series		Close Bid Ask Last	Total Vol Vol	Tot Op Int Op Int	Stock Series		Close Bid Ask Last	Total Vol Vol	Tot Op Int Op Int
Sep96	$29	2.50 2.75 2.65	50	50	Oct96	$65	1.10 1.35 1.15	10	10
	$30 p	0.15 0.25 0.15	65	345	**Methanex**		**$10.35**	180	8570
Nov96	$30	2.05 2.30 2.30	10	111	Sep96	$11	0.10 0.25 0.20	100	606
Feb97	$29 p	0.40 0.65 0.50	30	35	Oct96	$10 p	0.10 0.25 0.15	20	20
Cascades		**$5.80**	10	3222	Jan97	$11	0.35 0.50 0.40	60	60
Oct96	$6	0.15 0.25 0.30	10	357	**Midln Wlwy**		**$7.95**	31	1520
Corel		**$11.85**	233	6209	Dec96	$8	0.40 0.60 0.45	10	173
Sep96	$12½	0.40 0.60 0.50	33	81	Mar97	$8	0.60 0.85 0.80	10	20
Oct96	$15 p	3.05 3.30 3.15	25	172		$9 p	1.05 1.30 1.05	11	102
Jan97	$12½p	1.65 1.90 1.75	20	182	**Mitel**		**$9.20**	261	6173
	$15	0.70 0.75 0.65	12	783	Sep96	$7	2.20 2.40 2.05	10	639
	$17½	0.35 0.45 0.35	143	315		$9	0.45 0.50 0.45	70	1759
Cott		**$10.80**	72	6263		$10 p	0.90 1.05 0.95	5	15
Sep96	$10 p	0.25 0.40 0.25	50	300	Dec96	$8	1.55 1.75 1.35	10	320
Oct96	$12	0.40 0.50 0.40	7	177		$9	0.90 0.95 0.90	25	610
Dec96	$13	0.40 0.55 0.45	10	315		$10	0.45 0.55 0.35	120	411
	$13 p	2.55 2.80 2.50	5	1	Mar97	$10	0.70 0.85 0.65	21	66
Diadem Res		**$6.10**	291	3444	**Moore**		**$24.60**	61	987
Sep96	$5	1.25 1.45 1.40	20	517	Nov96	$25 p	0.80 1.00 0.85	10	95

SOURCE: THE GLOBE AND MAIL

TABLE XIII

as the exercise or strike price. These are the most popular variety, but there is another kind that gives you the same right in reverse. It is called a put option because you have the right to sell, or put, the underlying stock to the option seller at the agreed price.

You buy a call option if you think the price of the stock will rise. If you are right, the price of the option will also rise, frequently by a greater percentage, and you can sell it at a profit. Clearly, the legal right to buy a stock at a below-market price is valuable and the bigger the difference between the exercise price and the market price, the more valuable that right will be. A put option would be your choice if you believe the stock is heading downward. Again, if you are right, the option will rise in price as the stock price goes down. That's because the right to require somebody to buy the stock at a price above the going market price is also valuable.

Traditionally, stock options were bought and sold only on over-the-counter or unlisted markets. Option buyers usually realized profits by exercising the options they owned. Otherwise, they just let them expire. Before the introduction of exchange-listed options in the 1970s, it was difficult to find somebody else to buy your options if you wanted to sell them. Today, there are thriving markets in options on many stocks listed on major stock exchanges. A clearing corporation presides over these options markets. Its principal job is to guarantee the performance of every transaction by standing as the buyer to every seller, as well as the seller to every buyer. It also ensures that the number of options created by option sellers (known as writers) matches the number of options held by buyers. This could otherwise be a problem because there is no fixed limit on the number of options in existence. Options are not securities issued by a company, unlike stocks or rights or warrants. How many options exist depends entirely on the number of writers and buyers.

In Canada, all listed stock and index options are issued, guaranteed and cleared by the Canadian Derivatives Clearing Corporation, which is owned by the Toronto, Montreal and Vancouver stock exchanges. Its U.S. counterpart is the Options Clearing Corp. These agencies bring together the original writers of options with people who want to buy options. An option writer keeps the amount paid by the original buyer, known as the premium. In return, the writer takes the risk that some stock may be called away from him at a price below the market, or that some stock may be put to him at a price above the market.

A writer has to maintain a margin deposit with a broker as a sort of performance bond as evidence that he can meet his obligation to sell or buy the underlying stock. This is not a down payment, unlike the margin requested for ordinary stock transactions. Typically, it is also a smaller proportion of the total amount of stock that is being optioned.

Most options are not exercised, which can make option writing a profitable business. It is not, however, a business for small-scale investors. The safest form is practiced by owners of substantial portfolios of stocks who write call options against stocks that they already own and can therefore deliver easily if necessary. Writing so-called naked calls, where you do not already own the underlying stock, is a more perilous business. That's because you may be forced to buy a stock in the market at rapidly rising prices if that same stock is called away from you at a lower price. Writing puts is also a tricky business, best left to experienced and well-capitalized investors.

Index options provide another method of speculating on the market as a whole, if you really must. Suppose you expect the market in general to go up soon, but you are by no means sure about any particular stocks. It would be nice if you could buy a large enough portfolio of different stocks to make sure you owned the winners if your expectation came true. Obviously, this is impractical for most of us. Now, though, you can buy an option on just such a huge investment. In Canada, you can buy call or put options on a hypothetical portfolio made up of holdings of the 35 popular and representative stocks in the Toronto Stock Exchange 35 index. In mid-1996, the market value of that portfolio was about $7 billion. You could buy Toronto 35 call options for a few hundred dollars each at the time. To speculate on the U.S. market, you can buy an option on an even larger hypothetical portfolio made up of the 500 stocks in the Standard & Poor's 500 index.

Listed stock options and index options have many things in common. They can be bought and sold on the options market through your broker, just like a stock. To make trading easier, they have standardized expiration dates. The strike prices and other terms of the available options are also set by exchanges. The principal difference is that a listed stock option contract involves 100 shares, which is what is delivered if the option is exercised. So the exercise value of the stock option contract is always 100 times the price of the underlying stock. On the other hand, it is impractical to deliver all the stocks on which an index option is written, so the contract is expressed in terms of $100 rather than 100 shares. As a result, the exercise value of an index option contract is calculated as 100 times the index level and all transactions are settled in cash.

Like stock prices, the market prices of options reflect supply and demand. But figuring out the factors that influence options prices is even more complicated than assessing stock prices, and that's not only because the price of an option is frequently and mystifyingly called its premium, like an insurance policy. Here are the four key questions to ask.

Is the option "in the money," "at the money" or "out of the money"? These terms refer to the relationship between the option's exercise price and the market value of the underlying stock or index. Suppose a stock is selling at $30 and a call option is available with an exercise price of $25. You would expect the option to have a market price of at least $5, representing its intrinsic value, and it would be said to be in the money. The other way around (stock price $25, exercise price $30), there would be no intrinsic value and the option would be said to be out of the money. This does not mean the option's market price would be zero or a negative number, because of other factors described below. If the stock price and the exercise price are about the same, the option would be said to be at the money. Note that to evaluate a put option you must do everything in reverse.

How much time value does the option have? People buy an option because they expect something to happen before it expires. The further away that deadline is, the more chance there is that whatever it is will occur in time. Other things being equal, which they hardly ever are, an option loses its time value as the expiry date approaches. This sort of thing is what makes investing in stocks through buying options so tricky. Not only do you have to choose the right stocks, you have to get the timing right. However, you can now buy much longer-lived options than ever before. These options are called LEAPS, short for long-term equity anticipation securities, and have lives of more than two years in some cases.

Is the underlying stock or index frisky? If so, there will be seen to be a better chance of making money on an option and the price that investors will pay for the ride will normally be higher. Of course, it will also cost you more to climb into the saddle, but it may be easier to find others to take your place later on. A dull ride in the options market usually means losing your premium. Investors seeking a quiet life should look elsewhere.

Are we in a bull market or a bear market? When many stocks are rising in price, call options are usually a better bet than put options. In a declining market, it's probably wiser to buy puts or stay out altogether.

Options can be used defensively. Suppose you are in the happy position of having bought a stock that has soared in price. You would like to stay aboard in case it keeps going up, but you are getting worried about nailing down your existing profits while you still have them. As noted earlier, one way to handle this situation is to sell enough shares to take out your original stake and stay in the game using only your profits.

This still leaves your profits at the mercy of a sudden break in the stock price. However, if exchange-listed options are available on the shares, another manoeuvre is possible. You sell the shares and buy a call option, preferably one that is in the money, on the same number of shares. If your fears are realized and the stock goes down, you will be out the cost of the option, including commissions. If the stock keeps rising, you will still be around to share in the good fortune but with a much smaller stake at risk. You can keep buying new calls as the old ones expire for as long as it seems to make sense.

You can also use call options to buy a stock at today's price, even if you don't have the cash for the investment. In effect, you make a down payment on a stock you believe has a bright future, which you forfeit if things don't work out as expected. Again, if you believe a stock has a bright future but not with total confidence, you can buy a call option and put the money you saved into a safer fixed-income investment such as government treasury bills or savings bonds.

Put options can be used to sell short a stock that you think will go down soon. The advantages are that you don't have to put up margin money and the most you can lose is the cost of the put. Again, you can use put options to ensure against losing your profits on a winner. Just buy enough options to cover the number of shares involved and you will lock in your gains for the lifetime of the puts. Buy more puts as the old ones expire if you want to keep this insurance in force.

There are many more complicated and possibly rewarding ways to use options in the stock market, which you can investigate if you have the interest. A major drawback is that the commission bills mount quickly, a fact that leads some unscrupulous brokers to push options harder than they should. You will pay more to acquire a stock by first buying an option than by purchasing the stock directly, and the commission rate as a percentage of an options order is much higher than on a stock.

Suppose, for instance, you had bought 10 of those Bank of Montreal call option contracts, quoted at $1 each. The value of the order was $1,000 (10 times $1 times 100), and a typical commission would have been $100 or 10 per cent. In contrast, a typical commission on 1,000 Bank of Montreal shares bought directly would have been, say, $400, or 1.2 per cent on an order value of $33,000. Selling the option to nail down a profit would have cost another high commission. In effect, you would have to see the option price gain by more than 20 per cent before you were ahead of the game. Exercising the option and buying the shares would have meant paying the $400 commission on top of the $100. In most cases, however, that

$100 would be written off together with the $1,000 cost of the options, because roughly 90 per cent of exchange-listed options are never exercised.

This intriguing fact can make writing call options on certain stocks you already own an interesting and reasonably safe proposition. If such options are not exercised, you get to keep the premiums that hopeful investors paid for them, which can be a rewarding addition to your investment income. The mechanics are easily handled through your broker, but the key to success is to select carefully the stocks on which you write options. Your requirements are exactly opposite to those of the option buyer. Your biggest risk is to have shares called away from you because they have moved up in price, so you should choose safe stocks that do not move much, if at all. Then, most of the time, you will get to keep the stock and the option premium. Whether stocks that are unlikely to go up much are worth owning in the first place is open to question.

These days, you can also buy futures contracts on several stock market indexes, but you probably shouldn't. Remember that if you buy a futures contract and things go wrong, you can quickly lose much more than you paid for it.

The futures markets are for leverage junkies and for the professionals who use them to shift their risks to speculators. If you get involved in stock index futures, you will put up fairly small amounts of money for the chance to profit from price changes in remarkably large amounts of stock. The profits can come quickly if you are good at this sort of thing, or just lucky. The losses can come equally quickly. Be warned.

CHAPTER 16

Preferreds, Trust Units, New Issues and Unlisteds

COMMON SHARES THAT MAKE you part owner of a company are the staple diet of stock market investors. Buying them gives you a piece of everything the company has, including what it earns on the bottom line, but only after a lot of other people have taken their piece first. In effect, the owner of a common share stands at the end of the line if, for instance, the company goes out of business or suddenly doubles its profit. And what's left may be a lot, a little, or nothing at all, depending on how the company is doing. If it's little or nothing, you don't have any legal claim against the company because that was the risk you took. In return, you and the other common shareholders have the chance of sharing in a possibly huge jackpot if things go well.

This contrasts with the position of the company's creditors, who have a legal claim against it if they are not paid what they are owed, plus interest as agreed. Investors, for instance, may lend the company money by buying bonds in return for a promise of regular interest payments and ultimate repayment of the amount. If the company does not meet its obligations under the deal, those investors have the right to start bankruptcy proceedings to enforce their claims. They may also have the right to seize company assets to satisfy their claims. But if the company does well and meets its obligations with assets and profits to spare, those investors never get any more than what they are owed, plus the stated interest payments. The return on their investment is fixed from start to finish.

The distinction between the two arrangements is clear. However, there is a type of share sold by companies that muddies the waters considerably. It's the preferred share, in all its many forms. Owners of such shares stand somewhere between common shareholders and creditors. Like common shareholders, they are part owners of the company and they receive dividends out of profits. But they usually cannot look forward to a big bonanza if the company makes lots of money. Their dividend rate is usually fixed when the shares are initially sold by the company. It does not rise if profits rise. This means that preferred shares do not normally offer the potential for big capital gains offered to the owners of common shares. You buy these shares principally for dividend payments.

Yet, oddly, dividends on preferred shares are no more guaranteed by the company than dividends on common shares. Payments are entirely at the discretion of the board of directors and a preferred shareholder has no legal recourse if the company stops paying them. As a practical matter, the company usually tries harder to avoid cancelling preferred share dividends. Frequently, though, the sort of business misfortunes that lead to cancellation or "passing" of common share dividends force the company to stop paying dividends on preferred shares as well.

How, then, can the owners of such shares be said to have "preferred" status? First, if the company is wound up or dissolved, they almost always have a claim on the remaining assets of the company ahead of the common shareholders. The claim is usually for a fixed amount, and payable only after creditors' claims have been satisfied. Second, they usually have a prior claim to any dividend payments the company makes. In other words, the directors usually cannot pay dividends to common shareholders without first paying dividends on preferred shares. This often includes preferred share dividends that should have been paid in the past but were passed.

A medley of other conditions may or may not be attached to a particular issue of preferred shares, as set out in a company's charter. This is not a document that is easily available to investors, and such shares may not always even be described as preferred shares. They may have other designations such as "Class A." Most companies summarize provisions relating to preferred shares in the notes to the financial statements contained in the annual report to shareholders. Full details can be obtained from various sources such as the company reference information and annual surveys published by the Financial Post Information Service and from the prospectus that must be made available to investors who are buying newly issued shares.

Some of the conditions attached to a preferred share issue are there for the benefit of investors and some for the benefit of the company. Here are two examples of the kinds of provision that may benefit you.

A cumulative feature. This prevents the company from simply forgetting about unpaid preferred dividends. They have to be counted as arrears, and the company has to pay all those arrears before it can again start paying regular preferred dividends, pay dividends on its common shares or redeem preferred shares, that is buy them back for cancellation. Arrears payments are made to whoever owns the preferred shares at the time, so previous owners are out of luck. No interest is paid on arrears. However, an interesting profit can be made from buying preferred shares at a low price of a company that pays off its accumulated arrears soon afterward.

A purchase fund. The company promises to buy a specified amount of preferred shares on the open market each year, but only if they are available at or below a stated price. This promise provides support for the market price. A less attractive variation on this theme is a sinking-fund provision. The company sets aside a fixed amount or a percentage of earnings each year with the aim of buying back the entire issue of preferred shares over a period of time. As with the purchase fund, the company buys shares on the market only if they are available at or below the stated price. But there is an additional wrinkle: If not enough shares are available, the balance required is chosen by lot and called in compulsorily. Unlucky owners have to turn in a specified amount of their holdings and get a fixed price in return. This will usually happen when the market price of the shares is above the fixed call-in price, which means a loss for some shareholders. In each case, the shares purchased are cancelled, which reduces the total number trading on the market and improves the position of remaining owners.

Owners of preferred shares usually do not have voting rights. But many company charters give them the right to vote when a fixed number of dividend payments, or purchase or sinking-fund payments, are in arrears. Frequently, this does not mean much because there are usually fewer preferred shares than common shares. But it may mean something if a company in financial trouble proposes a major reorganization that requires a specified majority vote of each class of shareholder. Some companies also specify that one or more directors shall be elected by preferred shareholders in such circumstances.

The terms and conditions of a preferred share issue are usually quite difficult for a company to change without the consent of the holders, or at least a large majority of them.

The principal condition that is of benefit to the company is the call or redemption feature found in most preferred share issues. This gives the company compulsory-purchase rights over the shares at a price that is usually slightly higher than their original stated value, plus any unpaid dividends. Naturally, companies call in preferred shares when it is most convenient for them. Because investors buy preferred shares for the dividend income, their prices will usually rise when interest rates go down. It is at such a time that a company will see an opportunity to take advantage of lower interest rates by calling in higher-return preferred shares at a below-market price and replacing the capital with lower-cost money. Owners of the company's preferred shares will, therefore, see their shares taken away from them just when they are beginning to enjoy a capital gain.

Given this dismal prospect, plus the other disadvantages of preferred shares, why would any investor buy them? Usually, dividends paid on preferred shares are considerably higher than on common shares. But the main reason is the dividend tax credit. Preferred shares compete mostly with interest-paying investments, and interest income is fully taxable to most investors. So, of course, are dividend payments. But Canadian tax rules effectively mean that individual investors pay less tax on each dollar of dividends from a taxable Canadian company than on each dollar of interest. Dividend payments from non-taxable Canadian companies or from foreign companies do not get this special treatment.

This tax break takes into account the fact that dividends are not a tax-deductible expense to the company. They are paid out of after-tax profits, so it would hardly be fair to make dividend payments fully taxable again when the company passes already-taxed profits along to its shareholders. In contrast, interest is paid out of pretax earnings and is counted among a company's tax-deductible expenses as a cost of doing business. So it is reasonable for it to be fully taxable in the hands of the person receiving it. The dividend tax credit mechanism offsets double taxation, but only in an approximate way (see Chapter 18). The generosity toward individual shareholders that results enables companies to pay a lower pretax return in the form of dividends than when the payments are in the form of interest. A contributing factor is the rule that allows one taxable Canadian company to receive dividends from another taxable Canadian company free of tax. This market quirk occurs even though there is normally greater risk involved in buying preferred and common shares, and it's a prime example of how tax rules distort the financial markets.

Variations on the preferred share theme are available and attract some investors. Buy convertible preferred shares, for instance, and on top of the usually below-normal dividend you get the right to turn them in for new shares of the company, normally common shares. The conversion terms set an effective price on the common shares that is always above their market price at the time the preferred share is sold by the company. If the common shares were trading at, say, $22, the effective conversion price might be $25. This conversion privilege is available for a fixed period, typically five to 12 years. The conversion price may change according to a schedule fixed at the time of the original sale.

Redemption clauses are common with convertible preferred stocks. This means that the company is able to force you to convert if the market price of your preferreds rises above the redemption price. Faced with having your stock called away from you at a lower price, only a fool or somebody who is not paying attention would not take advantage of the conversion privilege. Converting does not cost a commission and you do not have to declare a capital gain or loss unless you sell the new shares you receive.

Another variation is the retractable preferred stock, which also provides a redemption option. On a specified date, you can force the company to buy back your shares at a fixed price, plus any dividends owing. There may be more than one date and retraction price. Remember that retraction does not happen automatically; it's up to you to make it happen if you want to get rid of your shares, another reason why you have to stay tuned if you buy preferreds. There are also preferred shares whose dividend payments go up and down in line with changes in interest rates, known as variable-rate or floating-rate preferreds. You may come across complicated examples of this variety. In addition, preferred stocks may come with warrants that allow the owner to buy new common shares at a fixed price for a fixed period of time. There are also participating preferreds that allow owners to share equally in the earnings of the

---

Calculating Preferred Dividend Coverage

$$\text{Coverage} = \frac{\text{Net income before extraordinary items} + \text{minority interests} + \text{current and deferred income taxes} + \text{total interest charges}}{\text{Total interest charges} + \text{total preferred dividends adjusted for income tax}^*}$$

$$^*\text{Dividend adjusted for tax} = \frac{\text{After-tax dividends} \times 100}{100 - \text{apparent tax rate}}$$

TABLE XIV

company, just like a common shareholder, but only after the fixed preferred dividend has been paid.

You can see that life as a buyer of preferred shares can get complicated. It is not a pursuit for the muddle-headed or for people who cannot be bothered to keep track of their investments. There is also the danger that you may get distracted by all the bells and whistles and forget the single most important issue: Is this company a good investment that is likely to keep paying its preferred share dividends? Nothing else matters much if the answer to that question is likely to be no. Your money will be safer if you stay well clear of a stock with such a question mark hanging over it.

There are actually three questions you should ask:

- Does the company make enough profit to cover the preferred dividends with an ample amount to spare?
- How long has it paid preferred dividends without interruption?
- Are there sufficient assets behind each preferred share, after deducting liabilities that must be met ahead of it?

The calculation of preferred dividend coverage is not a simple one. You take the net earnings before taxes, add back to that figure any minority interest, current and deferred income taxes and total interest charges. Then you divide that total by the total preferred dividends adjusted for income tax, plus the total interest charges. The adjustment is necessary because interest is paid before tax and dividends are paid after tax. The figure for the most recent fiscal year is important but, as usual, this calculation should be done for five fiscal years and the trend studied. A good broker can supply you with figures for a company whose stock you are considering. Many analysts suggest a rule-of-thumb minimum of three-times cov-

---

Calculating the Equity per Preferred Share

$$\text{Equity} = \frac{\text{Total assets} - \text{liabilities}}{\text{Number of preferred shares}}$$

Note: Some analysts deduct intangible assets, such as good will, from total assets. Use only those liabilities ahead of preferred shares.

TABLE XV

erage for typical industrial companies, that is, there should be $3 available for every dollar of dividends. This does not mean you should never touch the preferred stock of a company with less coverage. It's just that you should be aware of the risk and be sure you are getting some additional reward for taking it, such as a bargain price or high yield.

A company's dividend payment record can be researched through the company reference information published by the Financial Post Information Service and its dividend record booklets. The net assets behind each preferred share can be calculated from similar sources or from the company's annual reports. A shortcut check is possible through the independent credit ratings prepared by two Canadian companies, Dominion Bond Rating Service in Toronto and Canadian Bond Rating Service in Montreal. These companies publish rating codes based on a battery of statistical tests. A good broker can obtain these ratings and explain them to you. Remember, though, that the results of even such rigorous examinations depend partly on human judgment and intuition, as can be seen when the two firms assign different ratings to the same issue.

Convertible preferreds should be checked in the same way, but additional investigation is needed because of their relationship to a company's common shares. For convertible preferreds to be a promising investment, there should be a good chance that the company's common shares will rise substantially above the conversion price. There should also be a long enough time period until the conversion date to improve the odds for this to happen. If these factors are favourable, they may offset the generally lower dividends offered on convertibles, compared with ordinary preferreds. The convertible preferred shares will almost always pay a higher dividend return than the common shares, but the cost of acquiring the common

Calculating the Conversion Cost Premium and Payback Period

This example will show you how to calculate how much more it costs to buy a common share indirectly by buying a convertible preferred share first. It will also show you how long it will take to recover that difference from the higher dividend on the preferred.

1. Price of one XYZ Inc. $2 preferred share, which can be converted into 0.8 common shares, is $25.
2. Market price of XYZ common share is $22. If you multiply $22 times 0.8 you can see that the equivalent amount of a common share would cost $17.60.
3. Conversion cost premium is $7.40 ($25 – $17.60), or 42% ($7.40 as percentage of $17.60).
4. Years to pay back premium = $\dfrac{\text{\% premium}}{\text{Convertible yield} - \text{common yield}} = \dfrac{42}{8 - 4.6}$

$$= 12.4 \text{ years}$$

TABLE XVI

shares by taking the conversion route will almost always be higher than buying them directly on the market. One way to measure this trade-off is to figure out how long it will take for the higher preferred dividends to repay the higher cost of acquiring the common shares through conversion. It's a complicated calculation, as you can see from the example in Table XVI, but you may be surprised at the results when you apply it to a convertible preferred your broker is pushing. Frequently, if you like the company's common shares, you will be better off buying them directly instead of buying the convertible preferreds first.

Retractables present their own complications. The before-tax yield for a straight preferred is calculated in the same way as that for a common share — the dividend expressed as a percentage of the price. That calculation assumes no repayment by the company of the amount invested. So if a retractable preferred is selling at a market price higher than the retraction price, its yield is also calculated in the regular way because nobody is going to turn in shares under those circumstances. But if it is selling below the retraction price, a different method is used to reflect the likelihood that shares will be turned in at the first opportunity. This method takes into account repayment at the earliest retraction date and the length of time to that date, as well as dividend payments. It produces the so-called yield to maturity, or yield to first call. The math is complicated, but most modern financial calculators are programmed to make this calculation. Again, your broker should be able to supply you with the figure if you don't want to determine it yourself. But remember that the mathematical result means nothing if the company stops paying dividends in the meantime and is not in good enough financial shape to buy back your shares when the time for retraction comes.

A recently introduced investment vehicle is becoming a popular choice for investors seeking higher income payments, and who are temperamentally and financially able to take on some business risk to that income. What you buy are units in a trust specially created for this purpose. The trust receives a share of the cash earned from the production and sale of such natural resources as oil, natural gas, iron ore or coal. After their initial issue, the units are listed on a stock exchange and can be bought and sold like stocks. The trust pays out the income it receives, less some minor expenses, to owners of the units — usually quarterly, but monthly in some cases.

Although generally known as royalty trusts, there are actually two different types. One is the royalty trust itself. This type receives its income in the form of a royalty. Certain tax breaks given on natural resource production mean that for a number of years the trust's income is tax-sheltered. In turn, that means that the income paid out to its unitholders is tax-deferred. Unlike interest or dividends, that income does not have to be included in the investor's taxable income at the time. However, the distributions usually reduce the adjusted cost base of the units (see Chapter 18). This increases any eventual capital gain or reduces any capital loss that may eventually be realized.

The second type is more properly known as an equity trust. This kind of trust receives the income from natural resource production in the form of interest and dividends. In turn, the income it distributes counts as interest or dividends, depending on its source, and the unitholder is liable for tax on these payments each year according to the normal rules (see Chapter 18).

As income investments, the market value of both kinds of unit rises and falls in the opposite direction to interest rates, like preferred shares. Unlike preferreds, however, the income is not fixed. It always starts off high but it will fluctuate with the price of the natural resource involved. This is why these units should be classified as equity investments, not fixed-income investments.

The other thing to keep in mind is that the income you get comes from existing natural resource deposits. This means that in a sense part of the income is a return of your capital. This suggests you should look for an organization behind the trust with a good record of finding and developing new resources, or a trust with a claim on natural resource reserves stretching far into the future. Some notable examples of the latter are the Alberta oilsands and Labrador's iron ore.

If you want yet another change of diet or a change of diet from regular common shares, you can try new issues. This involves buying newly created common shares with money that goes directly into the company's treasury, after expenses, instead of buying already existing common shares with money that goes to the investor who owned them previously.

Companies sell new common shares to raise capital. Naturally, they try to make such transactions at the most favourable time for them, that is, when they can get a high price for their shares. This is a fact worth recalling when you are in danger of getting carried away with enthusiasm in a hot new-issues market. Typically, new issues of common shares appear in abundance only when a bull market has been going for a good while. In a bear market and in the early stages of a bull market, so few investors believe in a bright future that there is not much chance of an enthusiastic reception for new shares on terms that a company is willing to accept. Later in a bull market, more companies will find investors willing to pay acceptable prices for newly issued shares. And in the final stages of a roaring bull market, almost anything can be sold to gullible investors at prices that will later seem unbelievably expensive.

New issues do provide a general benefit to the market. They usually add to the amount of public information about a company. Securities law recognizes that investors can have difficulty in assessing the merits of new issues when the companies that sell them hire brokerage firms to market the shares and when much favourable publicity may be appearing. A company planning a new issue of shares is usually required to prepare and distribute to potential buyers a document, known as a prospectus, which accurately describes the company's operations, its financial history and much else. The idea is to ensure that sufficient information is available to allow investors to make an intelligent decision about the company's business prospects and the worthiness of its shares as an investment. Flights of fancy by the authors of the document are curbed by rules that make them and the company's directors legally liable for false or misleading statements. The wording of a prospectus is reviewed by government securities regulators, who from time to time will require it to be altered and can block the new issue until the company complies.

The acceptance of a prospectus by the securities regulators is not the same thing as a seal of approval of the company's shares as a good investment. It merely certifies that, in the opinion of the government's experts, all relevant information has been disclosed. It is still up to you to decide whether this information indicates that you are getting in on a good thing. As usual, you have to use the normal techniques of fundamental or technical analysis, or both, to decide whether you are looking at a bargain. Because you are dealing with a new issue, the odds are loaded against you and you should be even warier than usual.

A similar approach should be taken to considering an investment in shares traded only on the unlisted market, that is, shares not listed on any stock exchange. The principal advantage of investing in listed shares is their much greater visibility and easier access to information about them. In addition, to have their shares listed, companies must meet certain minimum tests of size and performance, although these are not guarantees that any particular stock is a good bet. Companies whose shares are not listed tend to be younger companies with uncertain prospects of success or survival, although there is a sprinkling of substantial, well-managed companies whose managements have decided not to seek a stock exchange listing.

There is no central physical marketplace for unlisted shares. Instead, they change hands through a vast electronic communications network linking brokers who specialize in these securities. These brokers act as principals, not agents, when trading unlisted shares. They own the shares they sell to you, and their profit or loss on a transaction depends on what they paid for shares when they acquired them. This differs fundamentally from most transactions on a stock exchange, where the broker earns his or her money by acting as an agent between the seller of the shares and the buyer.

The unlisted market system makes it difficult to know that you are buying or selling at the best price available at the time. Efforts have been made to improve things, however. In Ontario, the Toronto Stock Exchange operates the Canadian Over-the-Counter

Automated Trading System, known as COATS. This electronic quotation and reporting system provides current and historical information on prices and trading volumes. Reference information is also available about COATS-traded securities. Quebec has a system of collecting price and volume information on unlisted securities, which is made available to the financial press for publication the following day. But only a handful of quotations are published and no comprehensive statistics are easily obtained.

The much larger U.S. market in unlisted issues features the National Association of Security Dealers Automated Quotation trading system, known as NASDAQ. Dealers plugged into this system supply it with information on their transactions and price quotations. The accumulated information is published in daily and weekly financial papers. Various statistics on prices and volumes are publicly available, just like the statistics from the stock exchanges. There are also several price-measuring indexes.

Stocks of some very well-known U.S. companies are bought and sold through the NASDAQ system, and its volume of trading has become enormous. There is considerable controversy, however, about whether investors get a fair break from the brokerage firms that operate the market. In mid-1996, new fairness rules were under consideration by the U.S. securities regulators.

CHAPTER 17

An Investor's Guide to Foreign Affairs

CANADIAN INVESTORS PAY AS much attention to what is happening to the U.S. stock market as they do to the Canadian market. There are often minor differences in timing and the focus of attention, but by and large what Wall Street does today, Toronto and Montreal will also do today. If the Dow Jones industrials are doing well, Canadian investors will usually feel good, too. If not, the gloom will usually be shared north of the border, although the speculators operating on the Vancouver and Alberta exchanges often march to a different drummer.

The reason is simple: Canadian investors are right next door to the world's most influential financial market. What European and Japanese investors observe and feel from a distance, we observe and feel close at hand. In addition, the huge U.S. stock market offers a much wider range of investment opportunities than the Canadian market. Stocks of companies operating in industries that are just not available in Canada are lined up on Wall Street waiting to be taken for a spin. And you can buy and sell most of them in larger amounts than you can with comparable stocks in Canada. As the experts put it, the liquidity of U.S. listed stocks is usually much better.

U.S. securities regulators also oblige companies to make available to investors much more information than do Canadian regulators. Canadian financial journalists accustomed to digging out morsels of information from shy Canadian corporate executives find a dizzying array of facts, figures and opinions available if they go foraging south of the border. There are many more analysts following many more stocks in the U.S., and the results of their research can often be obtained through your Canadian broker.

Commissions charged on U.S. stocks and options are roughly comparable to Canadian. Some firms now charge exactly the same number of dollars on U.S. orders as on Canadian orders, but of course these will be higher-value U.S. dollars. But that comparison does obscure the fact that you will often pay considerably more commission on small U.S. orders. However, you will pay less on large orders because volume discounts are normally more generous in the U.S. For instance, on a $6,000 order for 200 shares at $30, Canadian commission at a full-service broker would be around $135; comparable U.S. commission would often be about $150 in more costly U.S. dollars. In contrast, on a $20,000 order for 1,000 shares at $20, the Canadian commission would be about $325 and the U.S. commission about $300. These differences are not too significant, though, if you consistently find more rewarding investments in the U.S..

All this being so, why should you bother with the Canadian stock market at all? Why not join the much larger group of investors from the U.S. and around the world who place their savings in the U.S. markets? There are two principal reasons. First, venturing into any stock market outside Canada involves taking on an additional major risk. To buy a stock listed on Wall Street, you have to pay in U.S. dollars. When you sell a stock listed on Wall Street, you receive U.S. dollars. And the value of those U.S. dollars, in Canadian currency, can change. For instance, in mid-1996 it cost roughly $1.37 in Canadian currency to acquire each U.S. dollar. That meant also that you received $1.37 Canadian, less the exchange conversion cost, for each U.S. dollar of profit you might have made on a stock on which you realized your well-deserved gains. In contrast, some 20 years ago you would have received much less, as little as 96 cents at one point.

This means that to do well in the U.S., you must get two difficult things right. You have to pick the right stock and you have to pick a time when the Canadian dollar is dropping in terms of the U.S. dollar, or at least not going up enough to wipe out any capital gains. By now, you know how difficult it is to choose the right stock. The currency timing problem makes everything that much tougher.

Second, tax rules are a handicap. The dividend tax credit that gives Canadian investors a break on dividend income (see Chapter 18) is available only on dividend payments from taxable Canadian companies. There is no such break on dividends paid by foreign companies, which lowers the after-tax return on their stocks. Yet, capital gains on foreign stocks are taxable in Canada according to the normal rules. In addition, there is a U.S. withholding tax on dividends paid by U.S. companies to foreign investors.

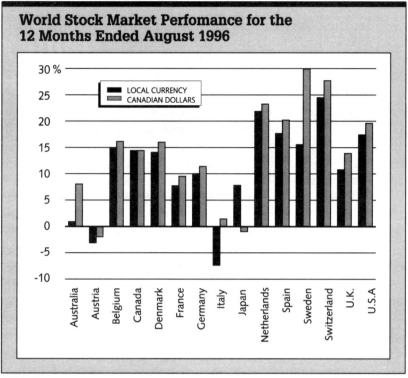

World Stock Market Perfomance for the
12 Months Ended August 1996

CHART XII

Also, only 20 per cent of the assets in a registered retirement savings plan can be placed in foreign investments. This severely restricts the amount you can put into foreign stocks through a self-directed plan. The calculation is made at the time you buy a foreign stock, by comparing the amount invested outside Canada with the total book value or tax cost of the investments in your plan.

These drawbacks apply equally to investing in stocks elsewhere in the world. But in far-flung markets, they are made worse by the difficulty of keeping a close eye on what is happening to your investment. A vast amount of news and commentary on U.S. stocks is easily available to Canadian investors. To follow overseas stocks closely is usually impractical, however, except for professional specialists. Quotations for some companies are listed in *The Globe and Mail*, *The Wall Street Journal*, the U.S. financial weekly *Barron's* and in the London *Financial Times*.

In any case, regulations that oblige companies with publicly traded shares to release information about their operations are much more lax outside North America. The annual reports of most over-seas companies are usually presented in a different format from those of Canadian and U.S. companies and are singularly uninfor-mative even to those investors who know their way around. That is the case even if you can surmount language barriers.

Actually buying an overseas stock directly can be as easy as pick-ing up the phone and giving an order to your broker. After that, it gets tougher. It may take months before you become a registered shareholder and start receiving information the company provides to its shareholders. Another difficulty is the high price quoted for many overseas stocks. Canadian and U.S. companies generally like to split their shares if they rise into high double-digit territory, so that instead of owning 100 shares at $75 each, you will suddenly find yourself owning 300 shares at $25 each. The idea is to keep the price of a standard transaction of 100 shares within easy reach of in-dividual investors. But many stocks of companies elsewhere in the world are rarely split. So you may find yourself able to buy only 10 or 20 shares priced at several hundred dollars or even several thou-sand dollars each. This can make increasing or reducing your in-vestment in that company more cumbersome.

Ever inventive, however, Wall Street came up years ago with the American Depositary Receipt, or ADR. This is a piece of paper that can be bought and sold on the stock market as a sort of proxy for a foreign stock. Usually created and issued by U.S. banks and trust companies acting as transfer agents in the U.S. for the companies in-volved, it normally represents a fraction of a share. Normal stock commissions are payable on ADR transactions. In addition, it costs more to buy the stock through its ADR than buying it directly be-cause the ADR's price will include an amount to cover the cost of its creation. The advantage of ADRs is that their prices and the vol-ume of trading can be followed easily by Canadian investors.

From all this you can see that investing in U.S. and overseas stocks is not for beginners. Unless you have special knowledge about a particular part of the world that you are sure will affect the prices of stocks of local companies, you should stay away from di-rect buying and selling in overseas markets, and perhaps even from ADRs. However, it's also true that the Canadian financial markets represent just about 3 per cent of world financial markets. So stay-ing at home will cut you off from roughly 97 per cent of the world's investment opportunities. Again, with the kind of downward spiral described by the Canadian dollar in recent times, it is a good idea for investors with substantial portfolios to put some of their assets into other currencies.

The answer to this dilemma? Mutual funds that specialize in international investing offer the best way to go. You can choose from funds that invest anywhere in the world and funds that concentrate on a particular country or region, then leave it to the professional managers to pick the most promising individual securities (see *Understanding Mutual Funds* by Steven Kelman).

CHAPTER 18

The Taxman Cometh

SHORN OF ALL THE DETAILS, there are two basic ways to profit from investing in the stock market: You can receive dividend payments from companies whose shares you own, and you can make a capital gain by selling shares to somebody else for more than you paid for them. Either way, like it or not, you have a financial partner looking over your shoulder. Canada's federal and provincial governments will frequently demand a piece of your profit from both sources. Your actual return on your investment is what you get to keep after you have paid whatever income taxes are due.

The pain of this is lessened in two ways, however:

• Increases in your material wealth from dividends and from capital gains are usually treated with a lighter hand by tax collectors than regular earned income from your paycheque.

• Because you can deduct losses and investment expenses from otherwise taxable income within certain limits, the governments share in your investment tribulations as well as your successes.

The smaller tax bite on dividends applies only on payments from taxable Canadian corporations. If you receive dividends from a U.S. company, you are out of luck, although you can usually deduct from your Canadian income tax any taxes you pay to a foreign government. The Canadian rules are meant to reflect, in a rough and ready fashion, the fact that dividends are paid out of after-tax profits. But note also that it is not necessary for the company to have actually paid income tax, merely that it is normally subject to tax if it makes a taxable profit.

The mechanism that delivers the break is known as the dividend tax credit. When you first encounter this peculiar creature, you may wonder whether it's really necessary to go at things in this roundabout way. There is no denying the bottom-line benefit for most investors, though. What you have to do first is "gross up" each dollar

Dividend Tax Credit Calculations

Canadian resident in federal tax bracket of 26% receives $1,000 in dividends from a taxable Canadian corporation. Here is how the dividend tax credit and after-tax income are calculated.

1. Start with actual dividend amount	$1,000
2. Gross up dividends by 25% ($1,000 X 0.25)	250
3. Calculate taxable dividend amount	$1,250
4. Calculate federal tax ($1,250 X 0.26)	325
5. Calculate federal tax credit ($1,250 X 0.1333)	167
6. Calculate federal tax payable (subtract credit)	$ 158

All provinces except Quebec		Quebec residents	
Federal tax payable	$158	Federal tax	$158
Provincial tax (e.g., 47%)	74	Federal abatement (16.5%)	– 26
		Federal tax	$132
		Provincial tax	$325
		Provincial credit	– $111
		Provincial tax payable	$214
Total taxes payable	$232	Total taxes payable	$346
Net dividend ($1,000 – $232)	$768	Net dividend ($1,000 – $346)	$654

Note: Federal and provincial surtaxes not taken into account.

TABLE XVII

of dividends received by 25 per cent and count the full $1.25 as part of your net income when you do your taxes. The $1.25 is called the "taxable amount of dividend." You then calculate what you owe the federal government in the normal way. The next move is to reduce what would otherwise be your federal tax bill by the amount of the dividend tax credit. This credit is 13.33 per cent of the grossed-up or taxable amount of dividend, or 17 cents in this case (13.33% of $1.25). Then, in all Canadian provinces except Quebec, you calculate your provincial tax by applying the correct rate to your net federal tax on the dividend income after it has been reduced by deducting the dividend tax credit.

Quebec does things differently. It runs its own separate system of income taxes. Quebecers still gross up dividends received and include them in their taxable income, then reduce their federal tax bill with the 13.33 per cent dividend tax credit. But they then reduce what they actually pay to Ottawa by a further 16.5 per cent of the net federal tax that would be payable in other provinces. The provincial tax payable on the dividend is calculated first by including the grossed-up amount ($1.25) in net income as calculated according to Quebec's rules. The correct tax rate is then applied, and finally a provincial dividend tax credit is used to reduce the provincial tax otherwise payable. This credit is 8.87 per cent of the grossed-up amount.

Usually, this involved process is not as bad as it sounds. Companies that pay dividends are required to send their shareholders an annual statement that shows the grossed-up amount and the dividend tax credit. You just slot the numbers into the appropriate boxes on your tax return and do the calculations as instructed on the form. It is also not necessary to understand clearly the mathematics that produces a lower tax rate on dividend income for most people, although it is instructive to follow a few examples through (see the example calculations on page 150). What you do need to absorb is the fact that the source of the income makes a big difference in the tax bill.

Capital gains, for instance, are taxed under quite different rules from dividends and other kinds of income. Investors have to include in their net income just three-quarters of net capital gains — that is, after capital losses are deducted. They then pay income tax at normal rates on the increased taxable income.

Clearly, this treatment gives you a break. It means that 25 cents of each dollar of capital gains made in the stock market is always free of income tax. The bottom line for investors is that you always get to keep more of dividend income and capital gains after paying your tax bills than you do regular earned income. How much more? Unfortunately, because of the unbelievable complexity of today's income tax rules, there is no single and widely applicable answer. The amount you pay in taxes varies with the amount of your taxable income from all sources, which determines your tax rate. In turn, that depends on which province you live in.

There are rough rules of thumb, though. Comparing dividends with interest is fairly easy. Each dollar of dividends is equivalent to roughly $1.30 of interest on an after-tax basis. In other words, to match each dollar of dividends after tax, you have to receive approximately $1.30 in interest. Comparisons of after-tax capital gains are more complicated. The 25 per cent exclusion is worth more to investors in a higher tax bracket, and there are variations in impact from province to province.

1996 Equivalent Pretax Yields

If you live outside Quebec and your marginal tax rate is 51.36%*, your equivalent pretax yields in 1996 would be:

Interest	Dividend	Capital gain
4%	2.98%	3.16%
5	3.72	3.96
6	4.47	4.75
7	5.21	5.54
8	5.96	6.33
9	6.70	7.12
10	7.45	7.91

*Median federal/provincial/territorial tax rate for taxpayers in the highest bracket.

If you live in Quebec and your marginal tax rate is 52.94%*, your equivalent pretax yields in 1996 would be:

Interest	Dividend	Capital gain
4%	3.07%	3.12%
5	3.84	3.90
6	4.61	4.68
7	5.38	5.46
8	6.14	6.24
9	6.91	7.02
10	7.68	7.80

*Combined marginal tax rate for taxpayers in the highest tax bracket.
SOURCE: RICHTER USHER VINEBERG

TABLE XVIII

Table XVIII provides some indicators. They show how much you had to earn in 1996 from various sources of stock market investments to produce a particular after-tax rate of return. For example, a person in a marginal tax bracket of around 51 per cent living outside Quebec gets an after-tax return of 3.89 per cent on interest of 8 per cent. To achieve the same after-tax return on dividends would require a pretax dividend yield of 5.96 per cent. Similarly, on capital gains, a pretax return of 6.33 per cent would be equivalent to pretax interest of 8 per cent. Similar but generally less generous breaks on investment income are given to Quebecers.

To sum up, a dollar of capital gains is frequently worth more after tax than a dollar of dividends, and a dollar of dividends is always worth more than a dollar of interest. But again that's not the end of the story, because the stock market adjusts to reflect these differences. Because taxable investors are willing to pay more for a dollar of dividends than for a dollar of interest, the market puts a higher price on an investment paying dividends than on one that pays interest. Looked at the other way around, investors are prepared to accept a much lower before-tax yield on a dollar that is invested in a stock primarily bought for its dividends than on a dollar invested in a term deposit or a bond. In mid-1996, for instance, the average yield on the stocks that make up the TSE utilities index was about 4.6 per cent. That compares with 7 per cent available at the time on five-year term deposits. This relationship would make no sense if income from these sources were not taxed differently.

Further complicating matters is the introduction of the alternative minimum tax, or AMT, a device that ensures that you cannot entirely escape paying tax on investment income even through the most ingenious and enthusiastic use of legitimate tax shelters. It's another illustration of the "heads I win, tails you lose" philosophy of the government in tax matters. It's also an area where you should probably seek advice from a professional tax adviser.

It works this way: First, you calculate your tax bill by the normal method. Then you calculate it under the AMT rules. To do so, you have to add back to your regular taxable income certain so-called preference or tax-shelter deductions you have taken. From the resulting amount you then subtract a basic exemption of $40,000 plus the gross-up amount on Canadian dividends (25 per cent, not 125 per cent). In its 1996 budget, Quebec proposed to cut the basic exemption to $25,000 for 1997 and subsequent years. You take 17 per cent of what's left as the minimum tax you have to pay, or 20 per cent in Quebec, and determine whether it works out to more or less than your regular tax bill. You have to pay whichever is higher. But there is a silver lining to the unhappy experience of having to pay the AMT. The approximate amount by which the AMT exceeds your regular tax bill can be carried forward for seven years and used as a regular tax payment in a year when your regular tax bill is larger than your AMT liability.

The more use you make of tax shelters, the more likely you are to have to pay the AMT. You can also get caught if you have large amounts of the tax-free 25 per cent portion of capital gains. For instance, you may find yourself liable for AMT if you save up your annual contribution room to registered retirement savings plans for

Alternative Minimum Tax Calculation

The AMT rules are particularly complicated for Quebecers. This example assumes John Smith, a Quebec taxpayer, earned $52,500 in 1996 from his job. In addition, he received $5,000 of dividend income ($6,250 taxable) and incurred a capital gain of $10,000 on the disposition of shares, 75% of which is taxable. John also bought a tax-shelter investment. He claimed deductions of $40,000 and interest expenses of $5,000 on this investment. Prior to the AMT, Smith would have been in line for a big refund.

His income tax bills:

Federal government*	$1,154
Quebec government	1,667
Total	$2,821

However, Smith was obliged to pay more than twice as much because of the AMT rules. The AMT calculation was as follows:

	Federal	Quebec
Taxable income	$21,250	$21,250
Tax-shelter deductions	40,000	40,000
Interest expenses	5,000	5,000
Non-taxable capital gains	2,500	2,500
Dividend gross-up	(1,250)	(1,250)
Adjusted taxable income	67,500	67,500
Basic exemption	(40,000)	(40,000)†
Net adjusted taxable income	27,500	27,500
Gross minimum amount	4,675	5,500
(17% federal, 20% Quebec)		
Less: Non-refundable credits	(1,445)	(1,589)
Quebec income tax reduction for		
low- and middle-income taxpayers		(122)
Alternative minimum tax	3,230	3,789
AMT carry-over	1,896	2,082

*Federal tax includes individual surtax and is net of abatement.
†Quebec proposes to cut this to $25,000 for 1997 and beyond.

SOURCE: RICHTER USHER VINEBERG

TABLE XIX

a few years, then make a large catch-up contribution in one year. Other preference deductions that must be added back to your taxable income include:

- Contributions to registered pension plans, registered retirement savings plans and deferred profit sharing plans.
- Half of the bonuses paid on Canada Savings Bonds.
- Tax-sheltered investments of various kinds, such as Canadian exploration expenses, but only to the extent that the tax deductions taken produce losses.
- Interest expenses related to such tax-sheltered investments.
- Quebec Stock Savings Plan deductions, for Quebec provincial taxes only.

This is a difficult area of tax law. Tax experts have so far been unable to develop any general rules of thumb for figuring out the impact of the AMT rules on investment decisions. The possible combinations of income, tax shelter deductions and other circumstances are so varied that each case must be figured individually. If you have substantial deductions in the above categories, you should work out your tax liability both ways, under the regular rules and under the AMT rules (see the example calculation on the previous page).

Normally, tax collectors consider sales of shares on the stock market as capital transactions producing a capital gain or a capital loss. If you trade frequently, however, and behave in ways that indicate your stock market activities are akin to operating a business, your income from selling at a profit may be considered fully taxable as ordinary income. Of course, your losses would then be fully deductible, which is some consolation. Circumstances that would be taken into account include:

- Owning many different stocks for short periods
- Special knowledge and experience of the stock market
- Much time spent studying the market and investigating purchases and sales
- Investing primarily with borrowed money
- Investing mostly in speculative shares that are unlikely to pay a dividend

The amount of your stock market capital gains and losses is always measured against something called the adjusted cost base of the shares. This includes both the original price and most additional costs of acquisition such as commissions, but not interest paid on money borrowed to make the purchase. In the case of a single purchase and sale, the calculation is simple. Just subtract the adjusted cost base of the shares from the proceeds, then deduct sales commission from the difference. The calculation becomes more complicated when, as frequently happens, you sell identical shares that were bought at different times and at different prices. It is then necessary to work out an average adjusted cost per share. You have to add the adjusted cost of all the identical shares you own, then divide the result by the total number of those shares. It's done like this:

1. Buy 100 Anderson Enterprises at $20 in September, 1990
2. Buy 200 Anderson Enterprises at $25 in June, 1991
3. Sell 300 Anderson Enterprises today at $25
4. Average cost is:

100 x $20	=	$2,000
200 x $25	=	$5,000
Total cost	=	$7,000
Average cost ($7,000 ÷ 300 shares)	=	$23.33

5. Capital gain = 300 shares x ($25–$23.33) = $501

There are some quirks to figuring your capital gains or losses in special circumstances.

Convertible shares: If you convert these shares, no capital gain or loss is figured at that time. But your adjusted cost base on an eventual sale of the new shares received will be the same as the original, and usually lower, cost of the convertible shares.

Employee stock options: Usually, shares are acquired below market price. If so, employees who exercise their options have to declare the difference as fully taxable employment income. However, the adjusted cost base of the shares acquired is the market value, not the actual price paid.

Warrants and rights: No tax consequences arise until these are exercised or sold. What happens then varies with how they were acquired.

1. If purchased directly, the purchase cost is added to the adjusted cost base, which also includes the commission cost and the exercise price.

2. If acquired free of charge from owning shares, the exercise price is included in the adjusted cost base of all the identical shares owned.

3. If acquired as a "sweetener" that forms part of a unit of new securities, such as shares or bonds, the warrant is considered free of charge, so the cost base of the shares or bonds equals the cost of the

whole unit. The cost base of any shares or bonds eventually acquired with the warrant is the exercise price.

Frequently, however, warrants and rights expire without being exercised. If they were bought on the market, you can then claim a capital loss equal to the purchase price. However, if they were acquired free of charge, no capital loss can be claimed.

Worthless securities: Suppose you buy a stock and it drops in price until it is worth nothing. Can you just pin it up on the wall and claim what you paid for it as a capital loss? No, you normally have to give it or sell it to somebody for a nominal price of, say, one cent a share. The transfer must be made in writing. However, if the stock has become worthless because the company has gone bankrupt, you are considered to have sold it for nothing, which triggers a capital loss automatically, and to have immediately repurchased it at a cost of nothing. This means that if you eventually sell it, the sale price less commission will be a capital gain.

These rules apply to shares acquired after Dec. 31, 1971, when the capital gains tax system was introduced. There are different and much more complicated rules for shares acquired before that date, and you should talk to a competent tax expert if you have to figure out capital gains or losses on such shares.

The cost of borrowing money to leverage your investments is recognized by tax collectors. The general rule is that interest paid on money borrowed to earn investment income is deductible, so long as any eventual investment profits are not exempt from taxes. This means that the interest charged by your broker on margin purchases of stocks is normally fully deductible. In the case of preferred shares, however, part of the interest cost may be disallowed if it exceeds the grossed-up amount of the dividend payments (125 per cent).

All of the above is just a summary of the tax laws that affect stock market investments. Knowing all the details is impossible, especially since the taxman keeps changing the rules in a never-ending battle to plug holes in his net. Even professional tax experts have difficulty keeping up with the state of play. You must, therefore, proceed with caution if you try to take advantage of the rules through some unusual strategy. Your best plan is to buy and sell stocks on the basis of their investment merits. Remember that even though it hurts to hand over part of your winnings to the government, you get to keep the rest.

With that in mind, here are some officially sanctioned methods of minimizing the government's take.

1. Timing of sales to produce capital losses. Suppose you own a stock whose price has fallen and you see little chance of it recovering soon. If you have capital gains, it may make sense to realize a capital loss now and use it to reduce the tax bill on your gains. The proceeds can then be reinvested in a stock with better prospects. You could also buy back the stock you sold if you begin to think it has a chance of recovery, but you must wait at least 30 calendar days or the loss on the sale will be considered a non-tax-deductible "superficial loss."

Remember that for tax purposes, ownership changes hands on the settlement date, which is usually three business days after the date of the transaction. This means that tax-loss sales must be made at least three business days before the end of the year to produce a capital loss in that same year. Do the deal closer to Dec. 31 and the capital loss will count only for the following year.

2. Tax-deferred investments. Deferring taxes on investment profits can put you ahead of the game for two main reasons. First, you can earn more profits on the money you would otherwise hand over to the government. Second, you may be in a lower tax bracket when the tax finally falls due.

Canada's premier vehicle for making tax-deferred investments, the registered retirement savings plan, is designed to take full advantage of both benefits, and adds a third break as well. Investment profits are not taxed as long as they are reinvested in the plan. The tax bill comes due only when it is cashed in, and you can defer that until the end of the year you become 69 years of age, and longer if you roll over the investments to a registered retirement income fund. Moreover, your annual contributions to the plan are tax-deductible within certain limits, so you are investing with before-tax dollars. Note, however, that the capital gains tax break and dividend tax credit are not available on stocks held in an RRSP. So capital gains and dividends are eventually taxable as ordinary income. This limits, but does not eliminate, the appeal of putting stocks in an RRSP.

You can have as many RRSPs as you like. To make tax-deferred investments in the stock market, you can choose mutual funds run by professional managers who invest part or all of the portfolio in stocks they choose. Going this route means you have only a limited influence over where your money is invested, which is probably a good thing if you do not want to take the time and trouble to learn do-it-yourself investing. Different funds have different investment philosophies, which they must describe publicly. So you can choose one that specializes in areas of the market that you like, one that specializes in foreign stocks or one that takes a conservative approach and has a diversified portfolio of blue-chip stocks. You can also switch your money from one type of plan to another, perhaps to one that does not invest in the stock market at all if you are worried about the outlook for stocks in general.

To have full control over the investment of your retirement savings you need to set up a self-directed RRSP. You can use these plans to invest in whatever you fancy, within limits set out in the tax rules. You decide whether to put all or part of the money in the stock market, or stay in bonds or mortgages. And you have the responsibility of choosing stocks for the plan's portfolio and deciding when to sell them, if ever. This is not a responsibility to be taken lightly. The trouble with tax-deferred and tax-sheltered investing is that the tax break can encourage you to lose sight of the object of the exercise: to make a good return on your investment. If things go wrong, the government may share in your losses but it doesn't underwrite them. You always lose something.

Going the self-directed route also means that you must have a good understanding of the limits imposed by the government on your portfolio. Stiff financial penalties await those who stray from the officially approved path. For instance, even though you may think Canada is the worst place in the world to put your money, you cannot put more than a specified portion of an RRSP portfolio into foreign investments. Until 1990, the limit was 10 per cent. Looked at the other way round, 90 cents of every tax-deductible dollar had to be invested in Canada. However, the limit was raised to 20 per cent over five years. For 1993, it was 18 per cent, and in 1994 it reached 20 per cent. The penalty: a tax of 1 per cent a month on the excess. There is one increasingly irrelevant exception. The penalty tax is not levied on foreign property acquired before June 18, 1971. Remember that the test is whether a company is incorporated in Canada, not whether it is foreign-controlled.

This rule restricts your investment freedom, although it may save you from yourself from time to time. It's tricky enough to pick stocks with good prospects in your own backyard, let alone venturing into foreign markets. Other restrictions can also be justified on the grounds that they prevent you from making what would normally be unsuitable investments for your retirement savings. For example, the perilous waters of U.S. unlisted stocks not quoted on NASDAQ are off limits. However, you can put unlisted Canadian stocks that are defined as public corporations under income tax rules into a self-directed RRSP, although it's probably not a good idea most of the time. Stocks listed on any of the five Canadian stock exchanges qualify, as do those listed on U.S. stock exchanges and on 14 other foreign stock exchanges, including Tokyo, London and Paris. Warrants and rights to buy RRSP-qualified stocks also qualify, and so do listed call options.

In general, shares of private corporations do not qualify, but there is an exception within limits for shares of Canadian-controlled private corporations resident in Canada that are not controlled by you or members of your immediate family. You can also avoid picking individual stocks by putting qualified mutual fund shares into your plan, but this means giving up some of the flexibility you sought through a self-directed plan. It's important for you to keep a continuous watch on the stocks in a self-directed RRSP to make sure they remain qualified investments. That status can be lost if a company goes private, moves outside Canada or if a merger leads to its shares being exchanged for securities that do not qualify under the rules. Like liberty, the price of safe tax deferral is eternal vigilance.

Obviously, self-directed RRSPs are not for stock market beginners. You have to pay an annual fee to the trust company or broker that provides them, currently $100 to $200. You also have to pay standard commissions on stock purchases and sales. You should probably not consider a self-directed plan if you have less than $15,000 to invest, and that amount should usually be put into mutual funds rather than just two or three individual stocks, in order to get a reasonable amount of diversification.

Stock savings plans of various kinds are available in several provinces. They are designed to encourage investment in shares of local companies, and the rules are usually skewed to favour smaller outfits. The breaks offered all reduce provincial tax bills, not federal taxes. However, rules vary from province to province and are changed quite frequently. Check with your broker to see if there is a plan available in your province.

CHAPTER 19

The Importance of Keeping Score

FLYING BLIND WITHOUT working navigational instruments is a dangerous business. So is investing blind, without proper records. If you are going to be a consistent winner in the stock market, it is essential to keep close track of what and how you are doing. First, you will need accurate and up-to-date records to keep the taxman happy and off your back. Second, you need good records to stay on top of the investments you have made, especially after you get beyond the one-stock stage. Third, you need dependable records to keep score. You need to know whether you are making or losing money from your investments before and after inflation, and before and after taxes.

You also need to compare the returns from your stock market activities with what you could earn if you put the money somewhere else. If, over several years, you find your profits from the stock market are much smaller than you could get from a less demanding form of investment, or if you are losing consistently, that might lead you to consider withdrawing from the game. True, you may still decide it's more fun making less money from picking stocks, but you will at least have made that decision in full possession of the facts, for whatever comfort that can give you.

When you buy your first stock, your broker may or may not confirm the transaction and the price right away over the telephone. In any case, a few days later you should always receive a written confirmation through the mail. If you don't get one within a week, call your broker. This document is the primary evidence of the transaction and you should keep it for as long as you keep your tax records. It almost always confirms that the deal went down just as you understood it would, but if it doesn't, get on the phone to your broker right away to sort things out.

The confirmation states, among other things, the date the order was executed, the number of shares or options or whatever is

A Sample Portfolio Report

Holdings	Security	Current price	Market value	% of total value	Indic. interest or dividend rate	Indic. annual income	% Yield
Cash & equivalents							
$10,000	CSBs	$100.00	$10,000	16.2	7.50%	$ 750	7.5
$20,000	T-Bills	$ 98.50	$19,700	32.0		$1,202	6.1
Total cash & equivalents			$29,700	48.2		$1,952	6.6
Marketable bonds							
$10,000	Can.'02s	$104.60	$10,460	17.0	8.50%	$850	7.83*
$5,000	Hyd.Que.'98s	$103.60	$ 5,180	8.4	8.75%	$438	7.99*
Total marketable bonds			$15,640	25.4		$1,288	
Preferred shares							
200	XYZ Series 1	$ 24.50	$4,900	7.9	$1.50	$300	6.1
Total preferreds			$4,900	7.9		$300	6.1
Common shares							
200	ABC Enterprises	$ 16.75	$5,025	8.2	$0.75	$225	4.5
500	DEF Technology	$ 5.45	$2,725	4.4	−		
200	GHI Mining	$ 18.25	$3,650	5.9	$0.55	$110	3.0
Total common			$11,400	18.5		$335	
Total portfolio			$61,640	100.0		$3,875	6.3

*Yield to maturity

TABLE XX

involved, the price, the commission and the total amount you have to pay. All this information will be needed when you eventually figure out the huge capital gain you hope to make on the purchase and the portion of your profit that you may have to give to the government. It is equally vital information if the deal goes sour and you are figuring out how much of your capital loss you can unload on the government.

At the end of a month in which there has been some action in your account, you will probably get from your broker a detailed statement of where things stand at that point. In more expansive days, brokerage firms used to provide customers with such a statement every month, even if there had been no activity. But these days many firms are shaving expenses by sending out statements for inactive accounts at longer intervals, usually every three months. During office hours your broker can always give you an up-to-date picture by calling up your account on a computer screen, although asking for this every day without ever placing an order will not make you a favourite caller. Some brokers also devise their own computer-generated reports to send regularly to good customers.

This information from your broker is one key source of what you will need to keep score of your investments. An equally key source are the daily or weekly quotations published in newspapers and specialist financial publications. These lists provide the market indexes and averages you will need to compare the performance of your stocks with how everybody else is doing. Key economic statistics are also available from newspapers and financial publications. You should always be especially aware of the current rate of inflation, which measures how quickly the purchasing power of each dollar is shrinking. If you make 5 per cent on your investments after tax, and inflation is running at 5 per cent, you are merely staying in the same place. This is better than falling behind by making less than 5 per cent, but making 10 per cent and getting ahead of the game would be better still.

These days, all of this sort of stuff is available from electronic services if you have access to a personal computer or the necessary special terminal. There are several Canadian and U.S. information services you can use to feed current market prices, trading volumes and other investment-related information over telephone lines to your machine. In some cases, the service will draw a chart of the stock or index you are interested in, right there on the screen in front of you.

This can be fun, but it's an expensive pastime. The fees and monthly connect charges will quickly swallow up a large slice of your investment profits if you are not careful. Taking data regularly from an on-line service is a luxury best suited to big-time players who buy and sell lots of stocks, to people whose employers pay the bills, or to those who find it an absorbing hobby. For the rest of us, and especially for small-time players with only a few stocks, it is cheaper and probably less complicated to collect the price quotations and other information ourselves, even if we then enter it manually into a computer.

Software is available at moderate cost to make the machine do the things it is very good at. These include remembering perfectly everything you tell it, doing accurately and in no more than a few seconds the calculations necessary to keep proper score, and reporting back to you everything you want to know about your investments except, alas, which stock to pick next. It's true that some people have written computer software that is said to provide reliable guidance on choosing stocks. This software is usually based on the techniques of either fundamental analysis or technical analysis. It may even help you to make up your mind now and then. Remember, though, no stock market guide, human or machine, is infallible. That's why doing the stock picking yourself is a good idea, as long as you pay close enough attention.

Records of your investment portfolio can be as elaborate as you wish or as simple as you can get away with, while still including the essentials. A portfolio report should have at least the following column headings:

- Holdings. The actual amount of cash should be listed. Cash equivalents such as Canada treasury bills and bonds should have their face value listed. Shares should be listed by the number owned.
- Security. Record the name of the investment. There should be separate sections for cash and cash equivalents, for bonds, for preferred shares and for common shares.
- Current price. This can be updated as frequently as you wish.
- Market value. For stocks, this is the current price multiplied by the number of shares owned. It is the principal measure of success or failure.
- Percentage of total value. The market value of each security should be calculated as a percentage of the total market value of the portfolio. Both the numerator and denominator in this calculation will change as market prices change, which is one reason why keeping these records on a computer will save a lot of time and effort.
- Indicated dividend rate. You can usually get this from the same place you got the price quotations.
- Indicated annual income. This is how much cash will come in over the next little while if you do nothing. In some circles, this is known as "unearned" income, but you know better. For stocks, you multiply the amount of the dividend by the number of shares owned. It's another good job for the computer.

• Yield. This tells you the percentage return on your investment that you are getting from the dividends on your stocks and from interest on other investments. This is calculated by dividing the actual dollars by the market value and converting the result into a percentage. Fire up a computer again, if you can, to figure out this constantly changing figure.

There are two practical advantages to using this fairly short list of column headings. First, you may be able to get them all on one sheet of wide paper, without using print so small it hurts your eyes. Second, they will concentrate your mind on the vital statistics you should be thinking about. In particular, you should always consider the current market value of the portfolio as your total investment, not what you paid for the securities in the first place.

This is a subtle, but very important, point. Suppose you made some good investments a while ago and your portfolio has doubled in market value. Certainly it's fine now and then to check out your original stake and gleefully count up the fortune it has turned into since. But you should always remember it's that whole fortune you have at stake in the market today, not just the original stake. You could cash in your chips at today's prices and spend the money on a world cruise, or pay off the mortgage, or set up a charitable endowment. Your decision each day not to do any of those things is just as much an investment decision as was your first stock purchase. This is why the yield on your investments is always calculated on the current market price, not on what you paid originally.

You can, however, expand your report so it gives you an immediate picture of your unrealized capital gains or losses, or perhaps keep track of them in a separate report. You will need to add a column for the purchase price, a column for the dollar gain or loss on your holdings, and perhaps columns showing the simple percentage gain or loss and the annual gain or loss.

If you want to get fancier still, you can keep records for each stock with information about its industry group, its level of risk, your price objective (where you think it has a fighting chance to go), your mental stop-loss price (the point below your purchase price at which you are going to think hard about ditching the dog), and who recommended the thing in the first place (it was probably your own idea). You can note the level of your favourite market index or average when you bought something, keep track of its changes and calculate how you're doing compared with the market. You will certainly want to keep count of the commissions you pay, for tax reasons. You add them to your original purchase cost, thus reducing your taxable capital gain or increasing your tax-deductible capital loss. And you deduct them from your sale proceeds, with similar effects.

With this information you can analyze your investment portfolio up, down and sideways. You can see how much of your savings are in low-risk or high-risk stocks. You can classify your stocks as inflation hedges or deflation hedges, and load up on one or the other according to how you figure the future is shaping up.

All of this sort of thing can be done with pencil and paper, preferably with the help of a cheap electronic calculator. It can also be done more speedily and conveniently using a computer and one of the personal financial software packages available from commercial sources. There are any number of U.S. packages that will do the job of record-keeping and analysis of your portfolio as well as keeping all your personal accounts, but the major differences in tax rules between the two countries may lessen their usefulness to Canadian investors. Good Canadian packages have also started to appear.

Remember also that if you are a Quebecker, a tax-preparation package designed for residents of other provinces will not be of use to you unless it has been adapted to your province's separate set of rules. Even a federal tax return for Quebeckers is different from those for the rest of Canada.

CHAPTER 20

Making Sense of the Future

IN THE MOVIE *BACK TO THE Future*, the young hero is transported through time to an earlier era and watches with amazement as his parents behave in embarrassingly juvenile fashion, unaware of the lessons that experience would later teach them. Just such amazement would result if an experienced investor from the present were transported to the middle of the 1970s to observe what investors were prepared to do at that time. Most notably, our time traveller would observe seemingly sensible people lending their savings voluntarily to governments and companies on terms that brought them little or no return after providing for taxes and inflation.

Indeed, for much of the time, it was actually costing them money. The dollars with which they were paid back were declining in value much faster than the rate of interest they were paid. The figures show, for instance, that in each of the five years from 1977 through 1981, investors holding long-term Canadian government bonds got back less from their investments than they had put in. The worst year was 1981, when the compound annual return on such bonds was -12.5 per cent, as calculated by the Canadian actuarial and pension consultant TPF&C.

That such perverse behaviour could continue for so long is a tribute to the ability of past experience to influence present actions. Those lenders allowed themselves to be robbed because of the memory of the happier years of the 1950s and early 1960s, when inflation was low and taxes more moderate, and savers could earn a reasonable real return without taking on the risks involved in buying stocks. The 1950s and early 1960s were also times that saw people who were prepared to venture into the stock market rewarded, by and large, with considerably higher returns on their savings than were available from lower-risk loans to governments and companies. In fact, this seemed the natural order of things — the greater the risk, the greater the reward.

Around 1980 to 1981, however, a revolution occurred in financial markets. Inflation appeared to be getting out of hand in North America. Lenders could be enticed only with steeply higher interest rates. In mid-1981, the Canadian government was briefly forced to pay more than 20 per cent on its three-month treasury bills, the short-term promissory notes sold to help pay the government's day-to-day expenses.

What this phenomenon told the observant was that people were no longer prepared to lose their savings to inflation. They began demanding high real returns for choosing to save some of their money, rather than spending it right away before the cost of everything went up again. Government bonds could be sold only in short-term deals of a year or two and most companies could not sell regular-style bonds at all.

Such a dangerous situation could not last for long, and it didn't. Resolute action by the U.S. and Canadian governments and their central bankers curbed inflation dramatically at the cost of a sharp economic recession in 1981-82. Moreover, when recovery began in 1983, inflation did not accelerate quickly again, as was widely expected. For the rest of the decade, the annual rate stabilized in the area of 4 per cent to 5 per cent, and it has since plunged even lower.

However, the memory of the 1970s inflation scare kept investors cautious. Interest rates required to sell government and corporate bonds came down, but not as much as inflation, which meant that savers began getting great deals. The amounts they were paid in interest put them well ahead of inflation and they also picked up some big capital gains on marketable bonds. That's because the market prices of previously issued bonds always rise as the interest rate required to sell a new issue falls. Clearly, if an already issued bond pays a fixed interest rate of 12 per cent on its original cost and today's new bonds pay only 10 per cent, the older bond is worth more to a buyer today than it was when it was first sold.

The years 1982 through 1986 were banner years for bond investors. In 1982, the total return (price changes plus interest) on the representative index of Canadian bonds calculated by broker Scotia-McLeod Inc. was a startling 35.4 per cent. The figure was 11.5 per cent in the following year, 14.7 per cent in 1984, 21.2 per cent in 1985 and 14.7 per cent in 1986. Oddly, though, few bond investors

Key Facts of Investment Returns

COMPOUND ANNUAL RETURN, INCLUDING INCOME

	1926-1995	Last 25 years	Last 10 years
Treasury bills	4.8%	9.3%	8.8%
Government bonds (long-term)	5.9	9.9	11.9
Stocks (TSE 300)	9.9	10.7	8.3
Inflation rate			
(compounded annually)	3.3	6.0	3.2

SOURCE: TOWERS PERRIN

TABLE XXI

appeared to enjoy those years. Most of the time they appeared to be consumed with worry that inflation would rob them of their gains once again.

Investors in stocks also did well in those years, but not as well as bond buyers. Moreover, the total return (price changes plus dividends) on Canadian stocks varied dramatically from year to year. Using the TSE 300 index as a measure, total return was just 5.5 per cent in 1982, 35.6 per cent the following year, -2.4 per cent in 1984, 25.1 per cent in 1985 and just under 9 per cent in 1986.

In 1987 and 1988, returns on Canadian stocks moved modestly ahead of returns on Canadian bonds and in 1989 the gap widened. The 1990 bear market pushed stock returns down sharply but briefly. Subsequently, however, returns on stocks improved again.

During 1993, investors in Canada and around the world enjoyed a very strong bull market in stocks. This suggested a more normal relationship is returning, although some sharp drops in prices during the first half of 1994 certainly slowed down the process. Towers Perrin figures show that over nearly 70 years from 1926 through 1995, inflation averaged 3.3 per cent annually, as measured by the consumer price index. The real total return (price changes plus income, less inflation) over that period averaged 1.5 per cent a year on the Canadian government's three-month treasury bills, 2.6 per cent on long-term Canadian government bonds and a much more rewarding 6.6 per cent on the stocks that made up the main price-measuring index of the Toronto Stock Exchange. However, the firm's statistical measures also show that the returns available on stocks varied much more from year to year than the returns available on treasury bills and government bonds.

It makes sense that, on average and over time, investors in stocks should make more on their money than they would from merely lending their money through buying bonds. That's because there is more risk in buying your average stock than your average bond. If people did not get a larger reward from investing in stocks, they would eventually stop doing so. If that happened, companies would not be able to raise risk capital and an important piece of the mechanism of the economy would permanently cease to work. This can, and does, happen for periods of time. But so far in modern industrial history it has not happened permanently, which is a good thing for all our sakes.

What happens in the financial markets, if they are left to work things out without too much interference, is that prices of bonds and stocks adjust to the changing circumstances. Remember that the return on your investment is calculated by dividing the actual dollars of income you get by the price you paid, with the result expressed as a percentage. So when prices rise, the investment return available to new buyers falls. At some point people stop buying and start selling. Then, as prices fall, the return available to new buyers rises until at some point it becomes irresistible again. This adjustment process is frequently obscured by the impact on day-to-day stock prices of changing investment fads and fashions, of greed and fear among investors, of wise and foolish acts by governments. But it is always there, and it works effectively.

None of this means, of course, that you can rely on always earning more return from a portfolio of stocks than from one made up of bonds or treasury bills. Nor does it mean that any particular stock is always and inevitably riskier than any particular bond. One thing worth remembering about averages is that if your head were in a furnace and your feet in ice-cold water, the average temperature over your entire body might well be in the comfortable range — but that fact would not do you much good in that predicament.

What it does imply is that no one should write the stock market off for the long run, even if at any particular time things look gloomy. Fear and foreboding are prominent features of the scene as we move further into a new decade, which is understandable. As of early 1990, the economy had had seven fat years in a row, which is a longer-than-average upward cycle. There was a widespread feeling that a lean year or two was overdue. And indeed a lengthy and painful recession followed. In their commendable efforts to prevent a rerun of the inflation scare of the late 1970s, it may be that the central bankers of the U.S. and Canada kept interest rates too high for too long in the late 1980s. Consumers were spent out and their credit was used up or at levels they could no longer tolerate. Because of the stock market's long rise, bargain-hunting investors found it tough to discover stocks that offered good value for their price. They found it much easier, though, after the 1990 bear market slashed prices.

In the wake of that bear market came a renewed bull market for stocks and bonds, as falling interest rates spurred the economy through 1992 and 1993. But early in 1994, the central bankers began raising rates once more, to slow economic growth that was considered too fast to last, and so head off a revival in inflation. Those rate hikes kicked the props from under the bond and stock markets during 1994, despite a powerful recovery in corporate profits. But by early 1995, it had become clear they had done their job as the economy paused for breath. So once again, interest rates fell and bond and stock prices rose.

At mid-1996, the big unanswered question was whether the central bankers had overdone it again and allowed the economy to accelerate in an unsustainable spurt, or had they successfully engineered a so-called soft landing — that is, slower but sustainable economic growth with low inflation, a sort of economic nirvana.

Meanwhile, the stock market had turned hostile to small-scale individual investors. Huge day-to-day and week-to-week swings in stock prices, associated with computer-driven trading by the professional money managers, made little sense to the rest of us. Far from making the market a more rational place, the computers appeared merely to have made it easier for the professionals to engage in the kind of mindless stampedes for which they readily criticize the small-scale investor.

Ironically but justly, it is becoming clear that the small-scale investor who ignores all this frantic flailing is the smart player. Choose your stocks well, diversify your risks, hold on tight for the ride, and the odds are good that you will cash out ahead of the game after, say, five years. In December, 1989, *Forbes* magazine published the results of a study that sought to throw light on the key question: Should the small investor boycott stocks just because they jump around in a scarier fashion than they used to? The answer was a definite no, which is significant coming from a publication that has often been critical of the investment industry and cannot be regarded as a mouthpiece for the business.

The magazine's researchers compared statistical measurements of daily price volatility in the stock market over the past decade with measurements of price volatility and total real returns on stocks for 60 overlapping periods of five calendar years beginning in the mid-1920s. The results showed that daily traders were really courting trouble. But five-year buy-and-holders enjoyed dramatically better odds of success. For a diversified shareholder, the risk of coming out with a real loss after five years was a little less than one in four. More striking still, the worst periods for losses were all long before computerized program trading was invented. The piece concluded that the highly publicized big price swings "are beloved of nightly newscasters, but of minimal importance to serious investors."

A recurring theme in this book is the need to march to your own drum if you are to win in the stock market. Remember the story about the fond mother who watched her clumsy son marching in the parade and shouted: "Look, our Willie's the only one in step." At some points in your investing career, you may feel lonely and out of step with everybody else because you have a view of the future that differs from that of the majority. It's much more comfortable being part of the crowd, even if you are all wrong together. The time you feel really foolish is when you differ with the crowd and you turn out to be wrong. That can happen, but surprisingly often it is the crowd that is wrong and the lonely contrarian who turns out to be the only one in step with reality.

As the 1990s began, for instance, the conventional wisdom was that the stock market was no place for a small-scale investor. There was too much danger of being trampled by the elephants, the multibillion-dollar financial institutions, as their professional investment managers rushed from one idea to the next, sometimes displaying an attention span of about 30 minutes. Indeed, individual small-scale investors fled the stock market in droves in response to widespread publicity about the antics of the professional crowd.

Yet this was probably just the right sort of time for independent-minded small-scale investors to be in the stock market. For one thing, there were so few rivals around. For another, those who invest smartly on a small scale do have some advantages over the gargantuan institutions. There is the advantage of manoeuvrability. Small-scale players can bide their time and nip into a stock at the right moment. They can also move out just as quickly when they wish, either because the idea worked out and they can take their profit or because it isn't working out and they decide to cut their losses. Institutional managers have manoeuvring problems similar to those of a captain of an oil tanker that needs many miles of sea room to alter course. Small-scale investors can also invest success-fully in companies with only a fairly small number of shares avail-able for trading in the stock market. The managers of huge institutional portfolios are effectively restricted to companies with a large number of shares trading in the market.

Individual part-time investors can also do well by buying and selling stocks of companies in businesses they know a lot about, perhaps because they work in the same sort of business. Employees of a publishing company can learn enough about that business to make intelligent judgments about which similar companies are worth investing in and which are not. The same goes for mining companies and supermarket chains and real estate outfits. An indi-vidual investor can do very well indeed by choosing a small number of stocks and getting to know everything worth knowing about those few companies. In time, he or she will acquire as much knowledge about chosen stocks as any securities analyst or portfolio manager, and maybe more. That's because the professionals usually have too much on their plates to put a major effort into any one stock.

Is it worth making the effort, in bottom-line terms? That partly depends on how much you are paid for your time already and on how much you invest in the stock market. If you earn $100 an hour or more at your day job and you have almost nothing to invest, it may not seem worthwhile to invest more time studying the stock market.

For many people, though, the payoff for success is well worth it. Take even a small starting portfolio of, say, $20,000, on which you can earn 6 per cent, or $1,200 a year, in interest without much risk. Instead, you spend a couple of hours a week studying companies and as a result you raise the return to 16 per cent or $3,200 a year. The additional $2,000 amounts to $19.23 an hour, not a bad profit on an interesting hobby. Remember that most hobbies cost you money, instead of earning some. Also, you should start earning much more per hour as your portfolio grows. What's more, if you are making the key calls yourself rather than relying totally on some highly paid adviser, you will get to keep more of your winnings and you will have the satisfaction of knowing it was all your own work.

The very best of luck and success in your self-reliant stock market career.

The Companies in the Major Indexes

The Toronto 35

The Toronto Stock Exchange introduced its first stock price index in 1934, and created the present composite index of 300 companies, the TSE 300, in 1977. The Toronto 35, introduced on May 27, 1987, consists of 35 of the most widely traded stocks on the TSE. In June, 1995, the Toronto 35 companies were:

Abitibi-Price Inc.
Alcan Aluminium Ltd.
BCE Inc.
Bank of Montreal
The Bank of Nova Scotia
Barrick Gold Corporation
Bombardier Inc. (Cl B)
Canadian Imperial Bank of Commerce
Canadian Occidental Petroleum Ltd.
Canadian Pacific Limited
Canadian Tire Corp. Limited (Cl A)
Dofasco Inc.
Imperial Oil Limited
Imasco Limited
Inco Limited
Laidlaw Inc. (Cl B)
MacMillan Bloedel Limited
Magna International Inc. (Cl A)

Moore Corporation Limited
National Bank of Canada
Noranda Inc.
Northern Telecom Limited
Nova Corporation of Alberta
Placer Dome Inc.
Renaissance Energy Ltd.
Rogers Communications Inc. (Cl B)
Royal Bank of Canada
The Seagram Company Ltd.
Talisman Energy Inc.
Teck Corporation (Cl B)
The Thomson Corporation
The Toronto-Dominion Bank
TransAlta Corporation
TransCanada PipeLines Limited
TVX Gold Inc.

The Dow Jones Industrial Average

The most widely used stock market average is the Dow Jones Industrial Average. It was first created in 1885 and tracked 14 stocks. The 30 blue-chip industrials of the DJIA today are:

Allied Signal Inc.
Alcoa of Australia Ltd.
American Express Co.
American Telephone & Telegraph Co.
Bethlehem Steel Corp.
The Boeing Co.
Caterpillar Inc.
Chevron Corp.
The Coca-Cola Co.
Walt Disney Co.
E.I. Du Pont de Nemours & Co.
Eastman Kodak Co.
Exxon Corp.
General Electric Co.
General Motors Corp.
Goodyear Tire & Rubber Co.

International Business
   Machines Corp.
International Paper Co.
McDonald's Corp. Inc.
Merck & Co.
Minnesota Mining
   Manufacturing Co.
J.P. Morgan & Co., Inc.
Philip Morris Companies, Inc.
Procter & Gamble Co.
Sears, Roebuck & Co.
Texaco Inc.
Union Carbide Corp.
United Technologies Corp.
Westinghouse Electric Corp.
F.W. Woolworth Co.

The Montreal Exchange Canadian Market Portfolio Index

The Montreal Exchange has published indexes of common stock prices since 1926, establishing its current indexes in early 1984. The ME Portfolio tracks the price movement of 25 blue-chip stocks on both the Montreal and Toronto exchanges. They are:

Alcan Aluminium Ltd.
Bank of Montreal
The Bank of Nova Scotia
Barrick Gold Corporation
BCE Inc.
Canadian Imperial Bank of Commerce
Canadian Pacific Limited
Canadian Tire Corp. Limited (Cl A)
Imasco Limited
Imperial Oil Limited
Inco Limited
Laidlaw Inc. (Cl B)
MacMillan Bloedel Limited

Moore Corporation Limited
Northern Telecom Limited
Placer Dome Inc.
Renaissance Energy Ltd.
Rogers Communications Inc. (Cl B)
Royal Bank of Canada
The Seagram Company Ltd.
Teck Corporation (Cl B)
The Thomson Corporation
The Toronto-Dominion Bank
TransAlta Utilities Corp.
TransCanada PipeLines Ltd.

A Glossary of Terms

ADJUSTED COST BASE is what the taxman figures a stock cost you for the purpose of calculating your capital gains or losses. This amount includes commissions, which are easy to calculate, and other items that are not — thanks to today's ridiculously complicated tax rules.

ADRs, or American depositary receipts, are pieces of paper that say their owner owns some shares of a big company based outside the U.S. They are traded on the New York Stock Exchange in U.S. dollars and provide North American investors with an easier way to buy and sell such foreign stocks than doing it directly.

BEARS are investors who believe that stock market prices are more likely to go down than up in the next little while. They may hold this pessimistic view about a particular stock or about the whole stock market.

BULLS are investors who believe market prices are more likely to go up than down in the next little while. They may hold this optimistic view about a particular stock or about the whole stock market.

CALL OPTION is a contract that gives you the right to buy a stock at a fixed price before a certain date. You buy one if you are convinced a stock is going up soon and you want to make a small bet pay off big by using leverage (see below). If you are wrong, the option will expire worthless, which most do.

COMMON SHARES are nicely printed pieces of paper, or more often entries in an electronic record-keeping system, that represent an ownership share in what the company owns after providing for its debts, and in whatever profit — if any — it earns after paying all its expenses. At least over the long run, they still seem to outperform safer investments but smart picks may even do well in the short term.

DIVIDEND YIELD is how much you are getting in dividends as a percentage of the amount you have invested in a stock. A $20 stock paying 80 cents a year has a dividend yield of 4 per cent. It's important always to work this out on the current market price of the stock, because today's price measures the amount you have invested. What you paid originally is merely a historical footnote.

DIVIDENDS are regular payments a company may make out of its profits to the owners of its shares, but there are no guarantees. If the company is losing money or its management wants to reinvest all the profits, there is nothing you can do about it except sell the shares — probably at a loss. One consolation is that your income from dividends is treated more generously by the taxman than your paycheque.

EARNINGS PER SHARE is how much the company is earning per share, not including extraordinary items that are beyond the control of management. It's the starting point in all assessments of what a company's shares are worth.

EARNINGS YIELD is how much the company is earning per share as a percentage of the amount you have invested in the stock. Again, work it out on the current market price. It is the mathematical reciprocal of the P/E multiple (see Price-Earnings Ratio) — that is, divide the multiple into one and you will get to the same number.

EX-DIVIDEND means that you don't get a previously declared dividend on a stock that you buy because you are too late to get on the shareholders' list in time. Instead, the seller receives the dividend. To give time for the preparation and distribution of dividend cheques, companies freeze their shareholders' list at some time before the dividend-payment date. Stocks in this no-man's land are marked with an X in the newspaper quotations tables. They usually drop in price by the amount of the dividend on the day they go ex-dividend.

LBOs, or leveraged buyouts, are deals in which a company is bought with a lot of borrowed money, often by its own management, on the premise that the repayments will be handled out of the company's own cash, including what it can get for selling off some or possibly all of its assets. Like most such bright ideas, in the bull market of the 1980s, the early deals made sense but many of the later ones didn't. Recently, LBOs appear to be coming back into fashion.

LEVERAGE is making one dollar do the work of many. There are many variations on the theme but all have one principle in common: Your profits will be magnified if you are right, as will your losses if you are wrong.

LIMIT ORDER is when you tell your broker to try to buy the stock at no more than $15, and preferably less. Alternatively, you may tell him to sell the stock for what you can get but not for less than $15. Use this sort of order sparingly or you may never get to buy or sell.

LIQUIDITY in the stock market can be good or poor. If it's good, that means there are enough shares of a particular issue available for trading so they can be bought or sold in reasonable quantities with small price changes between transactions. If it's poor, that means there are not enough.

MARKET ORDER is when you tell your broker to buy at the lowest price going, or to sell at the highest price possible. It's usually the best kind of order.

NEW ISSUES are stocks in private companies whose owners have decided to turn them into public companies. When you buy already-issued stocks, the money, less expenses, goes to the investor who sold it to you. When you buy a new issue, the money goes to the owners of the private company, after expenses. New issues can be hot — that is, rising quickly above the original offering price because everybody wants them. Or they are not, because nobody is panting to buy them. Buying a hot issue at the original offering price would make you a lot of money, if you could actually get some and you sell quickly while it's still hot. As for the other kind, this is one time when going with the majority view could save you money.

OPEN ORDER, also known as good-till-cancelled or GTC, is when you give your stockbroker a limit order (see above) that is valid until you cancel it. Don't forget about one.

PENNY STOCKS are stocks selling at disreputably low prices — that is, measured in cents instead of dollars. There are two kinds: those that were originally sold at such prices, and those that once sold at respectable prices but became penny stocks later on. As a rule, both kinds should be avoided unless you realize you are speculating, not investing, and you are doing it with money you can afford to throw away.

PREFERRED SHARES are nicely printed pieces of paper, or more often entries in an electronic record-keeping system, that entitle their owner to be paid a fixed dividend each year out of the company's profit. There is no guarantee the company will always pay the dividend, but at least you are in line ahead of the common shareholders because the company can't pay them without paying you first. Sometimes, companies sell convertible preferreds, which can be exchanged for common shares at a fixed price for a certain amount of time.

PRICE-EARNINGS RATIO is the price of the stock divided by the profit the company makes per share. A $10 stock of a company that is earning the equivalent of $1 for each of its shares has a ratio of 10. Also known as the P/E multiple, it's a measure of whether a stock is cheap or expensive. Bargain-priced stocks are often the best buys, but not always.

PROGRAM TRADING refers to huge computer-driven transactions in stocks and index futures by the professional managers of big pools of money. These transactions are supposed to ensure that they can't lose, whatever the market does. It hasn't worked out exactly according to plan and the practice is blamed by many people for the scary and violent price swings in today's stock market. Some folks even want it outlawed.

PUT OPTION is a contract that gives you the right to sell a stock at a fixed price before a certain date. You buy one if you are sure the stock's price is going down soon and you want a small bet to pay off big by using leverage. If you are wrong, the option will expire worthless, which most do.

RIGHTS are what you get if the company in which you own common shares decides to raise some capital by offering a deal to its shareholders. You get the chance for a short period to buy more shares from the company in proportion to your existing holdings, usually at a discount price. It can work out well if the company has a profitable use for the money.

SHORT SALE is when you sell a stock you don't own at today's price, because you believe the price will go down soon and you will be able to buy it back later at a profit. Your broker arranges to borrow the stock for you. You can make a lot of money doing this, but it's a tricky business. If you are wrong, and the price soars, you will have to bail out at a loss and sometimes it may be hard to get your hands on the stock at any price.

STOP-LOSS ORDER is when you tell your broker to sell the stock if it drops to a certain price. This can save you from big losses, but not always. That's because if the stock drops through that price like a falling rocket, the broker will sell you out at the best price available, which may be several dollars lower in such unhappy circumstances.

UNDERWRITER in the stock market means a brokerage firm or group of firms that has agreed to buy a new issue of shares from a company at a fixed discounted price, subject to some weasel clauses, and to arrange resale of the shares to investors in general at the full price. The underwriting profit is the difference between what the underwriter pays the company and what it gets from the investors.

WARRANTS are usually used by companies to make a sale of new bonds or shares more attractive. Normally, they are options to buy more shares in the company at a fixed price, but sometimes you get the right to buy something else such as a bond or a commodity such as gold. They are usually detachable after the initial sale and are traded separately. Unlike rights, their life span is one or more years.

Bibliography

There are three sorts of books about the stock market:

1. Basic textbooks, ranging from primers like this one to comprehensive and complicated volumes for further study

2. Classic accounts — which have withstood the test of time — of how people behave in the stock market

3. Current get-rich-quick books, most of which will not survive changing circumstances.

Only the first two categories are likely to be of much help to you. Here is a selection of such titles. Some have gone through a series of editions. The year of publication is for the most recent edition.

For further study:

How to Invest in Canadian Securities. Publisher: Canadian Securities Institute. A shortened version of the course offered by the national educational organization for the investment industry. Updated regularly.

The Canadian Securities Course. Publisher: Canadian Securities Institute. The text of the complete correspondence course offered by the national educational organization of Canada's investment industry. Updated regularly. The course is designed for would-be brokers but is available to the general public.

Security Analysis, by Benjamin Graham, David Dodd and Sidney Cottle. Publisher: McGraw-Hill (1962). A classic textbook on fundamental analysis. Details are out of date, but the principles remain relevant.

The Intelligent Investor, by Benjamin Graham. Publisher: Harper and Row (1973). A more easily readable distillation of the techniques described in *Security Analysis* and the author's long experience in the stock market.

Technical Analysis of Stock Trends, by Robert Edwards and John Magee. Publisher: John Magee (1966). A classic textbook on technical analysis. Examples and details are out of date but the principles remain relevant.

Secrets for Profiting in Bull and Bear Markets, by Stan Weinstein. Publisher: Dow Jones Irwin (1988). More current explanation of technical analysis by a leading practitioner.

For entertainment and instruction:

A Random Walk Down Wall Street, by Burton Malkiel. Publisher: W.W. Norton (1973). The author explains why most people who try to predict the market's moves usually get it wrong. A good book to read near the top of a bull market when you, like everybody else, have started to believe you are a genius.

Extraordinary Popular Delusions and the Madness of Crowds, by Charles Mackay. Published in 1841. A classic text on the mysteries of crowd psychology, it was highly recommended by financier Bernard Baruch, who claimed it had saved him millions. It will repay the time spent searching for a copy.

Famous Financial Fiascos, by John Train. Publisher: General Publishing (1985). An *Aesop's Fables* for the stock market investor.

Money Angles, by Andrew Tobias. Publisher: Simon and Schuster (1984). A rollicking collection of wonderfully written pieces on how things really are in the stock market, by one who has been there.

One Up on Wall Street, by Peter Lynch, with John Rothchild. Publisher: Simon and Schuster (1989). A witty, anecdote-filled book by a top mutual-fund manager on how to use what you already know to make money in the market.

Paper Money, by "Adam Smith." Publisher: Summit Books (1981). Wit and wisdom from George Goodman.

The Battle for Investment Survival, by Gerald Loeb. Publisher: Simon and Schuster (1965). A classic by a Wall Street insider who believed that the secret of success in the stock market was to put all your eggs in very few baskets, then watch the baskets closely.

The Money Game, by "Adam Smith." Publisher: Dell Publishing (1969). The hilarious but instructive book about the realities of the stock market that made George Goodman a star.

The Roaring '80s, by "Adam Smith." Publisher: Summit Books (1988). More up-to-date wit and wisdom from George Goodman.

The Wall Street Gurus, by Peter Brimelow. Publisher: Key Porter Books, Toronto (1986). A witty, informative and irreverent guide to how you can profit from investment newsletters.

Where Are the Customers' Yachts, by Fred Schwed. Published in 1940. A cynic's view of the stock market, presented with verve and venom. A good corrective to the more syrupy sort of advertising placed by brokerage firms.

Wiped Out, by an anonymous investor. Publisher: Simon and Schuster (1966). The funny-sad account of how one amateur investor lost a fortune in the stock market while the averages were making new highs. The book is dedicated to "my brokers, each and every one, whose capacity for self-delusion was commensurate with my own."

You Only Have to Get Rich Once, by Walter Gutman. Publisher: Bantam Books of Canada (1964). A classic by a Wall Street insider that describes how it takes more than knowing the numbers to be successful in the stock market.

The Globe and Mail Personal Finance Library. Publisher: The Globe and Mail. A series of books, including this one, that provides basic as well as in-depth information on every facet of managing your money.

Index

TO COMPLETE YOUR LIBRARY, ORDER ADDITIONAL TITLES TODAY!

THE GLOBE AND MAIL PERSONAL FINANCE LIBRARY

The Globe and Mail Personal Finance Library is designed to help you build your wealth and achieve your goals. Just a few minutes a day reading our books will give you you the insights you need to manage your money more effectively. To complete your personal finance library use this convenient order form.

Mail to: **The Globe and Mail Personal Finance Library, 444 Front Street West, Toronto, Ontario M5V 2S9**

Call: **1 800 268-9128** in Toronto: **416 585-5250**

Fax: **416 585-5249**

Visit: **Any bookstore that sells Penguin Books**

YES! *Please rush my order:*

☐ **SAVE 39%** Order the complete Globe and Mail Personal Finance Library Collection (11 books) for just **$109.99***

☐ 5 books for just **$55.99*** (a 30% saving)

☐ 3 books for just **$35.99*** (a 25% saving)

☐ Individual books are **$15.99***

☐ *The Only Retirement Guide You'll Ever Need* individual price **$19.99***

Call for special bulk pricing details.

Indicate your selection below:

____ Understanding Mutual Funds
____ RRSPs 1997
____ Investment Strategies
____ The Money Companion
____ Retire Right
____ The Gold Book
____ Bulls and Bears
____ Exploring Options
____ Investing for Income
____ Insure Sensibly
____ The Only Retirement Guide

Cost of books ordered	$	_____
* plus shipping & handling	$	5.00
* plus 7% GST	$	_____
TOTAL	$	_____

Name _____

Company _____ Title _____

Address _____ City _____

( ) – ( ) –

Province   Postal Code   Work phone # (include area code)   Home phone # (include area code)

Payment by   ☐ MC   ☐ VISA   ☐ AmEx   ☐ Cheque enclosed

Account Number |_|_|_|_|_|_|_|_|_|_|_|_|_|_|_|_| Expiry date (m/y) |_|_| |_|_|

Signature (required to validate order) _____